Matthew Segar, MD

The Physician's Job Search Playbook
A Strategic Approach from Interview to Offer

First Printing: 2025

ISBN-13 (paperback): 979-8-9927305-2-4
ISBN-13 (digital): 979-8-9927305-3-1

Printed in the United States of America

To Bayli and Milo

Contents

Preface

Why Your First Position Matters

The position you accept as a newly-minted attending physician will significantly shape your professional trajectory. This important decision affects not only your immediate earning potential and job satisfaction, but also your long-term skill development, networking opportunities, and professional reputation.

Selecting the right first position creates momentum toward a sustainable and satisfying career, while a poor choice can trigger burnout and disillusionment. As many experienced physicians observe, sometimes "less is more" when balancing certain professional trade-offs.

The skills and habits developed in your first position often determine your career direction, making these initial assignments particularly valuable. Job satisfaction doesn't just improve your daily experience—it enhances your career prospects and opens doors to a more fulfilling professional life.

This guide emphasizes thoughtful self-reflection and strategic planning as you evaluate your options for a first attending position. Your choice should align with your core values and set you on a path toward a rewarding and sustainable career.

How to Use This Guide Effectively

This book provides a comprehensive roadmap through the complex process of securing your critical first attending position. The content is organized to guide you sequentially through the major aspects of the job search process.

Chapter 1: Job Search Strategies introduces effective methods for finding positions, crafting strong application materials, and working with recruiters. This foundation helps you understand current market trends and how to position yourself effectively.

Chapter 2: Personal Branding and Professional Reputation explores how to establish your online presence, master in-person networking, cultivate your clinical brand, and protect your professional reputation—deciding elements for standing out in a competitive field.

Chapter 3: Understanding Physician Practice Models details the various employment models available, from solo practice to large healthcare systems, academic roles to telemedicine. Understanding these structures will help you identify which environment best aligns with your goals.

Chapter 4: Preparing for Interviews covers research techniques, presentation strategies, and questions to ask potential employers. The guidance on recognizing red flags during interviews and negotiations is particularly valuable for avoiding problematic situations.

Chapter 5: Compensation breaks down the complexities of payment models, billing basics, benefits packages, call pay, and malpractice insurance—ensuring you can evaluate the true value of offers beyond the salary figure.

Chapter 6: Contracts reviews key clauses to understand, red flags to watch for, and the importance of legal review. This chapter helps you navigate the legal aspects of employment agreements with confidence.

Chapter 7: Long-Term Financial Security addresses retirement planning, health insurance, and financial literacy basics to protect your future and maximize the value of your compensation.

Chapter 8: Medical Malpractice: A Primer explains the basics of malpractice, legal principles, protection strategies, handling curbside consultations, and what to do if sued—essential knowledge for practicing with confidence.

Chapter 9: Surviving and Thriving in the First 90 Days offers strategies for successful onboarding, time management, navigating workplace dynamics, and setting meaningful goals as you begin your new role.

The appendices provide practical tools, including a sample wRVU calculation and a contract review checklist to guide your decision-making process.

As you progress through this guide, approach it with your specific priorities and circumstances in mind. Use the chapters sequentially to build your understanding, or reference specific sections as particular needs arise in your job search process.

Setting the Stage for Success

Securing your first attending position represents a pivotal career transition requiring both clinical expertise and a clear vision for your future.

Start by examining your core values: What matters most to you? Autonomy? Security? Innovation? Patient-centered care? These values provide a framework for your career decisions, guiding your choices throughout the job search and helping align your career path with your long-term aspirations.

Next, take stock of your core competencies and skills. Be honest about areas for growth—continuous learning is essential for professional development. This self-awareness will not only inform your career choices but also prepare you to articulate your strengths and address your weaknesses during interviews.

Envision your desired future. What type of practice environment will let you thrive? What impact do you want to have on patients and the medical community? Setting measurable objectives and creating a deliberate career plan transforms your job search from a reactive scramble into a strategic pursuit.

Authenticity and self-awareness are perhaps your most valuable assets in this process. Aligning career choices with careful planning and informed decision-making allows you to confidently secure a position that will meet your personal goals and set you up for long-term success.

This guide will help you navigate each step of the journey—from identifying potential positions to signing your contract and thriving in your new role. The information and strategies presented here reflect both current industry standards and timeless principles of career management in medicine.

Chapter 1

Job Search Strategies

Entering the job market as a new attending physician is an exciting milestone, but it can also feel daunting. This chapter provides a comprehensive guide to effective job search strategies, crafting a strong CV and cover letter, working with physician recruiters, and preparing for interviews. It also includes sample interview questions with model answers, data on physician hiring trends, and warning signs to watch for during interviews and job negotiations. The goal is to equip early-career physicians with practical advice and confidence as they transition from training to their first attending position.

1.1 Effective Job Search Strategies

Finding the right job as a newly trained physician requires a proactive and strategic approach. Begin by **starting your search early** and using multiple channels to discover opportunities. Here we discuss where to find job openings, how to leverage professional networks, the role of physician recruiters, and timeline considerations for residents and fellows approaching graduation.

When and How to Start Your Job Search

Start Early: Don't underestimate the time needed to land the right position. The entire process – from initial inquiries to site visits, offer, and contract – often takes at least six to nine months.[1] This means final-year trainees should ideally start actively looking in the first half of their final

---

[1] NEJM CareerCenter Resources indicate that many residents underestimate the time needed for a thorough job search process.

training year. Many program directors and career advisors suggest residents start exploring opportunities about a year before completing training. Some residents even sign contracts in the summer before their final year of residency. While that early timeline is aggressive, it underscores the benefit of being proactive. At minimum, by the early fall of your final year (about 9–10 months before graduation), you should be sending out your CV or contacting potential employers, especially if you're in a less-recruited specialty or aiming for a highly sought-after city.

Your specialty and personal priorities can influence how early you need to start. If you have very specific geographic needs, dual-career considerations (e.g., a physician spouse also job hunting), or interest in competitive academic positions, plan for an even earlier start. For example, neurosurgery recruiters advise starting 12–18 months before completing training if targeting certain competitive niches. In general, **the more selective your criteria, the more lead time you should allow.**

Even if your specialty is in high demand nationally, delaying your search can limit your options or create a time crunch later on. Starting early also gives you time to compare multiple offers, negotiate, and handle licensing or credentialing requirements (which themselves can add a few months before you can start working). It's not uncommon for new physicians who waited too long to find themselves with a gap period after training. Avoid that stress by mapping out a timeline: for instance, research and networking 12 months out, applications and interviews 6–9 months out, and final negotiations 3–6 months before your availability date.

Where to Find Job Opportunities

New physicians can find job openings through a variety of sources. In practice, some avenues prove more fruitful than others, so it's wise to **cast a wide net** and use multiple methods:

Personal and Professional Networks: Your professional network is often the richest source of leads. Many physicians find their first job through referrals or word-of-mouth networking, such as recommendations from mentors, faculty, or senior residents you know. Let your attendings, fellowship directors, and peers know you are job hunting (if appropriate to do so), and ask if they have contacts in your desired region. Attend conferences or career fairs held by specialty societies – not only can you learn about openings, but you might meet future colleagues informally. Networking can also include alumni from your program or people you met during rotations and electives. In surveys, referrals and networking consistently account for a large share of physician hires (often 40–50%), making them the most common path to a job offer.

Online Physician Job Boards: Numerous job boards cater specifically to physician positions. These include popular sites like the NEJM Career-Center, JAMA Career Center, Doximity, Health eCareers, and specialty-specific job boards run by professional associations (for example, the American College of Physicians or American Academy of Pediatrics job boards). Many hospitals and health systems also post their physician vacancies on general job sites or LinkedIn. Job boards allow you to filter by location, specialty, and practice type. They are widely used – roughly one-third to one-half of new doctors use medical-specific online job boards in their search. Set up email alerts on a few major sites so you get notified of new postings in your field.

Hospital and Health System Websites: If you have target organizations or locations in mind, check those institutions' own career webpages. Large health systems often list physician openings on their sites under "Careers" or "Physician Opportunities." Applying directly through a hospital's website or HR department can sometimes get you into their applicant pool even for unadvertised or upcoming positions. This method accounted for about 9% of first-job placements in one survey (reflecting jobs found by contacting hospitals or facilities directly).

Specialty Journals and Newsletters: Don't overlook the old-fashioned approach of job ads in medical journals (print or online) and e-newsletters. For instance, journals like *New England Journal of Medicine* or *Annals of Surgery* often have classified sections for physician jobs. Specialty email newsletters or listservs may also carry job postings. While these are less commonly cited as the primary way doctors find jobs (often under 5–10% per surveys), they can still be a useful supplement to see a broad range of opportunities.

Recruiters and Staffing Firms: Physician recruitment firms are another major conduit for finding positions. Recruiters often advertise jobs on behalf of hospitals or private groups. You might see their posts on job boards or receive outreach from them directly. In some cases, working with a recruiter can give you access to openings not publicly advertised. Roughly a quarter of new physicians report using recruiting agencies or search firms as part of their job search. If you sign up on a staffing company's site or respond to a recruiter's inquiry, be prepared for frequent communication about potential jobs.

Locum Tenens Agencies: Taking a locum tenens (temporary physician) position can be a strategy for bridging to a permanent job or trying out different practice settings. Agencies like CompHealth, LocumTenens.com, and others list short-term assignments which sometimes convert to full-time offers if both parties are interested. About 14% of new physicians have done locum tenens work shortly after training – typically for reasons like exploring locations or as a stop-gap while seeking the ideal permanent role.

Social Media and Online Presence: Surprisingly, social media plays a relatively minor direct role in physician hiring. Platforms like LinkedIn, Doximity, Twitter, or Facebook can be useful to learn about organizations and connect with colleagues, but only about 1–12% of new physicians report finding jobs via social media. That said, ensure your online profiles (especially LinkedIn and Doximity) are up-to-date and professional; recruiters and employers will look at them, even if you don't actively job-hunt on those platforms. A clean, informative LinkedIn profile can complement your CV and might occasionally lead recruiters to you. Just don't rely solely on social media for your search.

Understanding the Role of Physician Recruiters

Physician recruiters can play a significant role in your job search – often reaching out to you before you even start looking. It's helpful to understand who they are and how they operate:

Who Recruiters Work For: In nearly all cases, physician recruiters are engaged and paid by the hiring organizations, not by job-seeking physicians. Hospitals, clinics, or medical groups hire recruiters (either in-house staff or third-party firms) to find candidates for their openings. This means that as a candidate, you typically do not pay any fees to work with a recruiter – their commission or salary comes from the employer side. Keep in mind, however, that because the recruiter's client is the employer, their ultimate goal is to fill the position successfully. A good recruiter will aim for a win-win match, but remember that they don't formally represent you in the way an agent might; you must still look out for your own best interests.

How and When They Contact You: Don't be surprised if your inbox and voicemail start filling up with messages from recruiters as you enter your final year of training. It's common to receive unsolicited emails or calls from physician recruiters as early as the last year of residency – sometimes even in the summer before that final year. Recruiters often obtain lists of graduating residents and will reach out to introduce themselves or pitch job openings. Many graduating physicians report receiving dozens if not hundreds of recruitment communications. In one survey, 56% of final-year residents said they had 100 or more job solicitations during training – an indicator of the high demand for physicians in many specialties. While the volume can be overwhelming, consider it an advantage that you're in demand. You can choose how much to engage with these outreach efforts.

Using Recruiters Proactively: In addition to fielding incoming calls, you can also reach out to reputable physician recruitment firms on your own. If you're targeting a particular region, for example, find out which recruiting firms work with hospitals in that area. Some well-known national physician staffing firms include Merritt Hawkins (AMN Healthcare),

Jackson Physician Search, CompHealth, Weatherby, Korn Ferry's physician division, and others. You might submit your CV on their websites or schedule a call. The key is to be clear in communicating your goals and constraints to any recruiter you engage. They can only help you find a good match if they understand what you're looking for (type of practice, location preferences, visa needs if any, etc.).

Hospitals' In-House Recruiters: Many large hospital systems employ their own physician recruiters. These individuals function like specialized HR personnel focusing on physician vacancies. If you apply through a hospital's career site, an in-house recruiter might contact you to schedule interviews. Treat them professionally and courteously (they often are your gateway to the decision-makers). Even though they work for the hospital, a good in-house recruiter will act as your point of contact, guide you through the process, and advocate internally on your behalf if you're a strong candidate. The dynamic is a bit different from third-party recruiters in that there's no "middleman" company – you are essentially dealing directly with the employer via their recruiter.

Preparing Your Application Materials Early

Even as you scout for job openings, make sure your application materials are polished and ready. Have an updated CV and a basic cover letter template prepared by the time you start contacting employers or recruiters. We'll cover detailed tips on CVs and cover letters in the next section. It's also wise to line up references (let your mentors or program directors know you'll be job hunting and ask if they're willing to serve as references or write letters). Being organized with paperwork – such as a personal statement (if needed), reference list, copy of your board exam results, etc. – can speed up your applications once you identify jobs of interest.

In summary, an effective job search strategy for a new attending physician combines early planning with diverse search methods. Start your search early, leverage personal connections, scan the major job boards, respond (selectively) to recruiters, and keep an open mind to different practice settings. By doing so, you maximize your chances of finding a position that fits your professional goals and personal life.

1.2 Crafting a Strong Physician CV and Cover Letter

Your curriculum vitae (CV) and cover letter are often the first impression you make on potential employers. A well-crafted CV and cover letter won't automatically land you the job, but they will help you secure interviews by showcasing your qualifications professionally and clearly. This section provides guidance on structuring your physician CV and writing an effective cover letter tailored to attending physician positions.

The Physician CV: Key Components and Tips

A curriculum vitae (CV) for a physician is a comprehensive record of your professional and educational accomplishments. Unlike a typical business résumé, which is usually kept to 1–2 pages, a physician's CV can be longer since it includes detailed listings of your training, experience, publications, and other credentials. However, longer doesn't always mean better – the goal is to be thorough yet concise and easy to read.

Core Sections of a Physician CV: While formats can vary, most physician CVs should include the following sections in reverse chronological order (most recent first within each section):

1. **Contact Information:** At the very top, list your full name, degrees (MD/DO), phone number, professional email address, and current address. You may also include a LinkedIn profile or Doximity profile URL if you have one (optional). Make sure your email address and voicemail greeting are professional.

2. **Education and Training:** List your medical training in detail. This typically includes your medical school (with degree and graduation year), residency (specialty, institution, years), and fellowship if applicable. You can also include significant post-doctoral research training or other formal programs here. Include undergraduate and other degrees as well, though the focus will be on your graduate medical training. It's usually not necessary to list high school. For each entry, list the institution name, location, your degree or position (e.g., *Resident, Internal Medicine*), and dates (year-range).

3. **Board Certification and Licensure:** List the certifications you hold (e.g., *Board Certified in Internal Medicine, American Board of Internal Medicine, 2025*) and any state medical licenses (active or pending, with license numbers optional). If you haven't yet taken your boards or are scheduled for it, you can indicate **Board Eligible** and the expected exam date.

4. **Clinical Experience or Employment History:** This section may be brief for a new graduate (since you've been in training), but you can include prior clinical employment (e.g., moonlighting, prior careers, or significant physician assistant/nursing experience if you had any), and leadership roles in training such as chief resident year. For each position, list title, organization, and dates. If you have gaps or non-clinical work, you can include it if relevant, but you generally don't need to list unrelated part-time jobs from long ago.

5. **Academic Appointments (if any):** If you've held any teaching or academic positions (even volunteer clinical instructor roles or teaching assistant roles during residency), list them here with institution and dates.

6. **Research and Publications:** Include any research experience, especially if it's relevant to the job or specialty. Under subheadings, list your peer-reviewed journal publications, books or chapters, abstracts, and significant presentations. Use a standard citation format (you can often use the format from PubMed or journal style for publications). If you don't have publications, it's not a problem – focus on other strengths – but if you do, make sure they're listed and up to date. For a new physician, it's fine if this section is short; include whatever scholarly work you've done, and if none, you can omit the section.

7. **Honors and Awards:** If you were elected to Alpha Omega Alpha (AOA) or Gold Humanism Honor Society, or received residency teaching awards, scholarships, or other honors, list them with years.

8. **Professional Memberships:** List memberships in professional societies (e.g., *American College of Physicians, American Academy of Family Physicians*), including any leadership roles or committee work in those organizations.

9. **Volunteer Service and Community Involvement:** Many employers appreciate physicians who are engaged in community or volunteer work. Briefly list significant volunteer activities, especially those related to healthcare or community service, with organization names and dates.

10. **Skills or Certifications:** Here you can list special skills (e.g., fluent in Spanish, proficient in medical French) and any additional certifications relevant to your specialty (ACLS/BLS are assumed for most hospital-based roles, but if you have ATLS, PALS, Neonatal Resuscitation Program, etc., you can list them). You can also note technical skills like specific procedures you're trained in (for example, OB/Gyns might list da Vinci robotic surgery training, or a family physician might list obstetric ultrasound competency).

11. **References:** It's generally acceptable to state "References available upon request" rather than listing individuals' contact info on your CV. If you do list references, provide 2–4 names with titles and contact information. Just ensure those people have agreed to serve as references for you.

CV Formatting Tips: Strive for a format that is clean, consistent, and easy to skim. Use a simple, professional font (e.g., Times New Roman, Arial,

Calibri) and avoid excessive colors or graphics. Most physician employers are fairly conservative, so stick to black text on white background, and use bold or caps to clearly label section headings (Education, Research, etc.). Use reverse chronological order within sections so that your latest achievements are seen first. For example, under Education, list fellowship, then residency, then medical school. Under publications, list the most recent first. Keep bullet points or description sentences to a minimum; your CV can be mostly an outline of facts. The content should be concise: brevity and clarity are valued. Even though a CV can be multiple pages, avoid dense paragraphs of prose – if you need to describe a research project or leadership role, one or two brief lines is sufficient (you can always expand during an interview). Make sure to proofread meticulously; there should be no typos or grammatical errors. A typo in your CV or cover letter can signal lack of attention to detail.

Tailoring and Maintenance: As a new physician, your CV will evolve quickly. Update it regularly (at least every few months during job search) to add any new licenses, publications, or accomplishments. You generally don't need to highly tailor the CV for each application – your CV should stand on its own as a complete record. However, if you're applying to a specific type of job (say, an academic position), you might emphasize your research and teaching sections by placing them earlier or adding more detail there. Conversely, for a pure clinical community job, you might put clinical experience and skills up front.

One strategy is to have a "master CV" with everything, and you can selectively trim less relevant sections if needed for a particular application (for example, removing an old poster presentation if you have many, or abbreviating sections to highlight what that employer cares about most). In general, though, physicians aren't expected to customize CVs as much as some other fields; your cover letter and interview will allow you to highlight specific relevant strengths.

The Cover Letter: Making Your Case

Your cover letter is a one-page letter that accompanies your CV when you apply or inquire about a job. Think of the cover letter as the narrative that ties together the key points in your CV in the context of the job you're seeking. A good cover letter personalizes your application to a specific position and conveys enthusiasm, fit, and professionalism.

Keep it Concise and Focused: A cover letter for a physician job should be no more than one page, typically 3–4 paragraphs. Recruiters and department chairs are busy; they appreciate brevity. Aim for a professional, positive tone that is also warm (not overly stiff). Absolutely ensure the letter is error-free – grammar, spelling, and names/titles must be correct.

Address the Letter Appropriately: Whenever possible, address your letter to a specific person – usually the physician leader or the recruiter in charge of hiring. If a job listing gives a contact name (e.g., "Please send CV and cover letter to Jane Smith, MD, Chief of Cardiology"), address it to that person. If you're not sure, a generic but polite salutation like "Dear Hiring Committee" or "Dear Dr. [LastName]" (if you know at least the department chief's name) is better than "To Whom It May Concern." Showing that you took the time to find the appropriate contact is a small but meaningful touch.

Opening Paragraph – Who You Are and Why You're Writing: Introduce yourself briefly and state the specific position you're applying for. Example: *"I am a third-year internal medicine resident at XYZ University, writing to express my interest in the hospitalist position at ABC Hospital (Job ID 12345) as advertised on your website."* If you have a personal connection or a strong geographic tie, you can lead with that: *"As a Houston native returning home after training, I am excited to apply for..."*. The opener should grab attention in a positive way and summarize in one sentence who you are (a soon-to-be graduate of X program in Y specialty) and what you're seeking.

Middle Paragraph(s) – Why This Job and Why You: Next, explain why you're interested in this particular position and how your background makes you a good fit. Do your homework on the employer so you can mention specifics. For example: *"I was drawn to this opportunity at ABC Clinic because of your reputation for innovative primary care delivery and the team-based approach highlighted on your website. During residency, I sought out rotations in ambulatory quality improvement, which sparked my interest in working at an organization that values continuous improvement – something I know is part of your culture."* Then, highlight a few key accomplishments or skills from your CV that align with the job: *"In addition to my clinical training, I have developed strong teaching skills as a chief resident, which I hope to continue by contributing to your medical student clerkships."* Tailor these points to what the job posting mentions. Be specific about the practice, location, or population – show that this isn't a generic form letter. If you have a connection to the area or facility (like you grew up nearby or have family there), mention it, as it demonstrates genuine interest and likelihood to stay. Overall, this section should answer: "Why do I want this job, and what do I bring to it?"

Closing Paragraph – Next Steps and Thank You: In your closing, express enthusiasm and a willingness to discuss further. For example: *"Thank you for considering my application. I would welcome the opportunity to discuss how I could contribute to your team. Please let me know if there is any additional information I can provide. I look forward to the possibility of an interview."* End with a professional sign-off: "Sincerely," and your name. If you will be in the area or attending a conference and could meet, you might note that as well ("I will be attending the ACS conference in October and would be happy to meet then").

Tailoring and Tone: Importantly, write a separate cover letter for each job – do not use a one-size-fits-all letter or simply change the address. Employers can spot a form letter easily, and it comes across as lack of interest. It's fine to have a basic template (your intro and main points might be similar), but always customize at least a few lines to show you researched that specific employer. Mention something about their facility, mission, or the community. The tone should be confident but not arrogant. You want to "market" yourself, highlighting what makes you unique, but also convey that you're enthusiastic about them. Avoid just rehashing your CV in prose form; the reader has your CV for details. Instead, pick out 2–3 strengths or experiences that align with the job and emphasize those.

Common Mistakes to Avoid: Don't focus on what you want out of the job ("I need a position that will advance my career"); focus on what value you offer and why you're interested. Also, avoid mentioning compensation or benefits in the cover letter – those discussions come later. Do not include negative comments about any past experience or make any demands. Keep it positive and forward-looking. Finally, keep the letter professional in format: if emailing, you can attach it as a PDF with your CV or write it in the body of the email (with proper letter format). Either way, include a subject line that makes clear you are applying for a position.

Have Others Review It: It's a great idea to have a mentor, faculty member, or career advisor review your CV and cover letter. They can provide feedback on content and catch any errors. Also consider the perspective of a hiring committee: does your letter make them want to meet you? A little extra time polishing these documents can make a difference in getting noticed.

In summary, a strong physician CV is comprehensive, well-organized, and easy to read, highlighting your training and credentials relevant to the job. Pair it with a thoughtful cover letter that connects your background with the specific opportunity you're pursuing. Together, these documents present a professional first impression that can open the door to interviews.

1.3 Working with Physician Recruiters: Tips and Pitfalls

Physician recruiters can be incredibly helpful in your job search – or a source of frustration if expectations aren't managed. This section provides insight into how to effectively work with recruiters, what to expect from them, and how to avoid common pitfalls in the process.

How Physician Recruiters Operate

As mentioned earlier, physician recruiters generally represent the hiring organizations. They come in two main types:

In-House Recruiters: These are employees of a hospital or clinic network, working in the HR or physician recruitment department. They focus on filling the needs of that specific organization. If you're communicating with a recruiter who has an email address @hospitalname.org, for example, that's an in-house recruiter. Their job is to shepherd you through that hospital's hiring process if you're a potential fit.

Third-Party Recruiters (Search Firms or Agencies): These recruiters work for independent firms contracted by hospitals or medical groups to find candidates. They often represent multiple job opportunities across different employers. They might reach out to you with a generic "I have a client in need of a gastroenterologist in the Southeast" or you might contact a firm saying "I'm looking in the Midwest, do you have any positions?" These recruiters often work on commission (paid by the hiring institution when a placement is made) or on a retainer basis. They often have broad knowledge of the job market and can present you with options from various employers.

Recruiters' Motivations: A good recruiter truly wants to make a successful match – one where both the physician and employer are happy – because that reflects well on their professional track record. They can be allies and advisors to you, providing information about the job market, salary expectations, and feedback on your CV. Some recruiters will even give you coaching for interviews or tips on your contract negotiation, since they want the deal to go through. However, it's important to remember that recruiters ultimately answer to the employer. Some recruiters may be very hands-on, while others take a more transactional approach (simply forwarding candidates). You are not obligated to go through a recruiter for a given job if you find another route, but note that if a recruiter first introduced you to a job, they are typically "attached" to that potential placement.

What to Expect: When a recruiter contacts you about a job, they should be able to provide basic details: the location, practice setting (hospital-employed, private group, academic, etc.), and highlights of the position (for example, "community of 50,000, offering $250K base salary plus RVU bonus, outpatient only clinic," etc.). Often, early conversations with recruiters are exploratory. They may ask about your timeline, your ideal practice, and what's important to you. Feel free to be candid – this helps them filter opportunities. You can also ask them questions about how many physicians have they placed at that organization before, or why the position is open (is it growth or replacing someone?).

Recruiters might not have all the answers, especially regarding day-to-day job details or workplace culture. In fact, one limitation is that recruiters might not know the nuanced realities of working in a given practice – they may not be able to judge a "bad workplace" or specific work-life balance issues. Use them for the facts and process, but do your own due diligence on the qualitative aspects.

If you engage with a recruiter, you can expect them to handle a lot of logistics. They often help schedule interviews, coordinate travel if it's an onsite interview (sometimes the employer covers your airfare/hotel and the recruiter helps arrange it), and act as a go-between for paperwork. Some employers channel all communication through the recruiter during the initial phases – meaning you might not talk directly to the hospital's HR until later. This is normal in many cases. Recruiters can also be useful in obtaining follow-up information – for example, if you had an interview and weeks have passed, a recruiter can nudge the employer or give you updates. They want to keep things moving.

Tips for Working Effectively with Recruiters

Be Honest and Open with Your Preferences: When a recruiter asks what you're looking for, be honest about your must-haves (like geographic region, practice type, visa requirements, etc.) and your nice-to-haves. Don't say "I'm open to anything" if in reality you have strong preferences – that could lead to wasted efforts on both sides. Conversely, if you truly are flexible, let them know the range of options you'd consider. The more a recruiter understands your priorities, the better they can match opportunities. For example, if work-life balance or certain schedule considerations are top priority, tell them that upfront.

Ask Clarifying Questions: Feel free to ask recruiters direct questions about the job or the hiring process. They can often provide valuable data like typical salaries in that region, competition for jobs, or insight into how quickly you need to act. If a job posting is vague, ask the recruiter for details (patient volume, call schedule, makeup of the group, etc.). A good recruiter will try to get you answers or at least tell you what they don't know.

Maintain Professional Communication: Treat all communications with recruiters as professional interactions – they are not casual chats with a friend (even if you develop a friendly rapport). Be responsive to emails or calls within a reasonable time, or politely tell them if you're not interested in a particular lead. If you agree to an interview set up by a recruiter, follow through or give ample notice if you need to cancel/reschedule. Your behavior reflects on you, and recruiters do communicate with employers about your professionalism. Also, keep records of which jobs each recruiter has discussed with you to avoid confusion or duplicate submissions (you wouldn't want two different recruiters accidentally pitching you to the same employer, which can create a messy situation).

Leverage Their Expertise: Recruiters often have a bird's-eye view of the job market. You can ask them things like, "What are you seeing in terms of compensation trends for my specialty?" or "Do you think my CV has any gaps that I should address?" Some recruiters will give feedback or even help polish your resume. They might also advise you on interview prep specific to that employer, or what the employer is really looking for in a candidate. Use them as a resource – it's in their interest to help you shine.

Stay in Driver's Seat: While you should listen to a recruiter's suggestions, remember you are free to pursue any opportunity through any means. You are not bound to only jobs a particular recruiter shows you. If you find a job on your own or through another recruiter, that's fine – just be transparent if needed (for instance, if a recruiter calls you about a job you already applied to directly, let them know you've engaged through another route to avoid confusion). Recruiters know doctors will have multiple leads; just keep the communication clear. Also, if a recruiter keeps pushing a job that you know isn't a fit, it's okay to politely but firmly decline and refocus them.

Understand the Recruiter's Role in Offers: In some cases, especially with third-party recruiters, they might serve as an intermediary during the offer and contract stage. They may even present the offer to you on behalf of the employer or handle some negotiation messages. If so, ensure you clearly communicate your questions and concerns to the recruiter so they can relay them accurately. Don't be shy about asking for what you need – whether it's clarification of duties or more competitive pay. However, note that recruiters typically do not make final decisions; they convey information. You should eventually get to speak directly with the employer (e.g., hospital HR or department leadership) about contract specifics, but recruiters can facilitate those talks.

Potential Pitfalls and Cautions

While many recruiters are professional and helpful, be aware of some potential pitfalls:

Misaligned Incentives: Because recruiters are paid by the hiring institution (often via a commission when a doctor signs on), there is a potential conflict of interest – they might be more motivated to close a deal than to ensure it's the perfect job for you. The vast majority want you to be happy too (since an early quit or a bad fit reflects poorly), but just keep in mind that you should double-check anything that feels like a sales pitch. If a recruiter seems to be glossing over potential downsides or pressuring you to accept quickly, take a step back and make sure you have all the facts.

Bait and Switch Scenarios: Although rare, a few physicians have reported situations where a recruiter advertised a dream job that either didn't materialize or turned out very different (e.g., "Oh, that position is no longer available, but let me tell you about this other one..."). If a recruiter contacts you about a job and after you express interest it suddenly changes drastically (or "disappears"), be cautious – it could be an anomaly or a sign the recruiter was just fishing for your resume. Use your judgment and don't give sensitive personal info unless you're confident of legitimacy.

Exclusivity and Contracts: Normally, you do not sign any contract with a recruiter as a candidate. If a recruiter ever asks you to sign an exclusivity agreement (saying you'll only work with them) or asks you to pay them, that's a red flag. Standard practice is that you are free to work with multiple recruiters. However, it's wise not to have too many people submitting you all over; focus on one or two trusted recruiters to avoid overlap. If a recruiter submits you for a position, typically another recruiter cannot submit you for the same one – you are "claimed" in that process. So if you are working with multiple recruiters, ensure they are presenting you to different opportunities.

Overcommunication or Spam: Some physicians feel inundated by recruiter contacts – daily calls or emails can be distracting. It's okay to set boundaries. You can tell a recruiter your preferred contact times or methods. If you feel a recruiter is not respecting your limits (e.g., calling your personal phone at odd hours repeatedly), you might choose to cease engaging with that person. There are plenty of recruiters out there; work with those who act professionally.

Incomplete Picture of the Job: As mentioned, recruiters may not know everything about a job's conditions. For example, a recruiter might accurately describe the compensation and requirements, but they might not know that the last three doctors left due to management issues. That's why you should use the recruiter to gather official info, but also do independent research: talk to physicians who work or have worked there if possible, and pay attention during your interview for any red flags. Recruiters won't intentionally hide known issues, but they might not be privy to them either.

Negotiation Dynamics: Recruiters can facilitate negotiation, but make sure you advocate for yourself. Studies have shown some physicians (especially women) are less likely to negotiate salary offers, possibly to their detriment. Don't let the presence of a recruiter stop you from negotiating as needed. If the recruiter is presenting the contract, you can go over each point with them. It might feel awkward to negotiate through a middleman, but it's normal. Just be clear on what you want; a good recruiter will carry that to the employer. And you can always request to speak directly with the hiring manager or HR for detailed negotiations if you prefer.

In essence, working with recruiters can expand your reach and streamline your job search, as long as you stay informed and assertive. Many new attendings successfully find their first jobs with the help of recruiters. Use them as advisors and connectors, but continue doing your own homework on each opportunity. By maintaining open communication and a bit of healthy skepticism, you can harness recruiters' efforts to your advantage in finding the right position.

1.4   Job Market Trends and Hiring Statistics

To close this chapter, it's useful to understand the landscape you're entering as a new attending. The physician job market has its own trends in terms of demand, hiring practices, and timelines. Knowing these can help set your expectations (for how long your search might take, for example) and guide your strategy.

Overall, the demand for physicians in the United States remains high. A long-predicted physician shortage – especially in primary care and certain specialties – is materializing as population needs grow and older physicians retire. For context, even as residents are swamped with recruiter messages, healthcare organizations are struggling to fill positions. Recent data show that primary care physicians (like family medicine, internal medicine) are among the most sought-after, with nearly three-quarters of organizations actively recruiting in those fields[2]. Other high-demand areas include hospitalists, emergency medicine, OB/GYN, psychiatry, and many surgical subspecialties. Rural and underserved areas in particular face shortages; positions in these locations may offer higher salaries or loan repayment incentives to attract candidates.

As discussed, networking and referrals are golden. A survey of early-career physicians found that 40% obtained their first job through personal referrals or networking contacts. The same survey noted that about 12% were offered a job at the site of their training program (so don't discount your residency or fellowship institution if you like it – many programs hire their graduates). Roughly 10% found jobs via medical-specific job boards, and smaller percentages through recruiters or direct outreach. Interestingly, social media was a negligible source of actual job hires (around 1%), despite wide use for searching. The takeaway: make sure your mentors and professional network know you're job hunting, as that's often the most effective route to find a position.

Timeline to Hire: How long does it usually take to land a job? It varies,

---

[2]9 Key Takeaways from AAPPR's 2023 Benchmarking Report

but averages can be illuminating. On the employer side, the average time to fill a physician vacancy is on the order of 4–6 months (120–180 days) or more [3]. For primary care, one report cited ~125 days to fill, and ~135 days for specialists. Some highly specialized roles take much longer – even up to a year to get a signed contract. And after signing, onboarding (credentialing, licensing, privileging) can add another 4+ months before the physician actually starts. This underscores why residents are advised to sign contracts well before graduation – many aim to sign by the winter of their last year of training for a summer/fall start, which aligns with that 6-month lead time.

From a physician job-seeker perspective, a survey by the Association of American Medical Colleges found about one-third of residents had secured a job by more than 6 months before finishing training, and roughly another third by 3–6 months before, with the remainder getting jobs closer to or after graduation. It often depends on specialty and personal circumstances. More than half of graduating physicians now begin their job search at the start of their final year of training, which has moved up compared to past generations. The average resident or fellow might interview at several places and have multiple offers to consider. So, while the market is competitive in some popular urban areas, newly trained doctors are in demand across much of the country.

Geography and "Lifestyle" Roles": Certain locations (e.g., desirable metropolitan areas with many physicians) remain more competitive. If you have your heart set on a very specific city where there are few openings, expect to put more effort or be patient. Conversely, if you're open to a wider region or smaller communities, you may find an abundance of options. Another trend is the rise of "lifestyle" positions (like hospitalist shifts, urgent care, telemedicine) which can offer more predictable hours. These are popular among new physicians valuing work-life balance, and employers have expanded these roles. The COVID-19 pandemic also expanded telehealth opportunities; some physicians are doing part-time telemedicine in addition to clinical jobs.

Employment vs. Private Practice: The job market has shifted heavily toward employed positions. About 90% or more of new physicians are opting for employment by a hospital, health system, or large group, rather than solo or small private practice. This is both due to personal preference (guaranteed salary, less administrative burden) and the reality that fewer small practices are hiring straight out of training without partnership track. Many specialties (like emergency med, anesthesia, radiology) are typically group-based or employed models now. That said, if your goal is to become a partner in a private practice, those opportunities exist but often involve an employed period followed by partnership buy-in. Be sure to ask about the partnership track (length, buy-in amount, what ownership entails) if that's

---

[3] Trends 2025: The future of physician hiring | Healthcare Finance News

a route you consider – it's a common pathway but varies widely. Academic jobs often involve an employed faculty appointment at a set salary (with potential research/teaching responsibilities). And there's always the locum tenens or independent contractor path as an alternative for those who want more flexibility early on.

Compensation Trends: Salaries for new attendings vary by specialty and region. Organizations like MGMA publish annual physician compensation data which show that surgical and procedural specialties tend to earn the highest, primary care and pediatrics on the lower end, with internal medicine subspecialties in between. The good news is physician salaries have been gradually rising in most fields (though some adjustments occurred around COVID). If you're curious, sources indicate, for example, family medicine average starting salaries might be around $240k, hospitalist $300k, general surgery $350k, anesthesia $400k, etc., with wide ranges. Many jobs now use productivity-based models (like RVUs or bonus) in addition to a base salary, even for new grads. Understanding those models is important (and asking for transparency in how they work, as we'll note in red flags). You might also encounter signing bonuses, relocation allowances, and loan repayment offers – these are common sweeteners, especially in high-need areas. For instance, a rural primary care job might offer a $50k sign-on and medical school loan assistance.

Trends in Contracts: Most new physicians are starting on 2-3 year contracts with clauses for renewal. Non-compete clauses are still common in many contracts (meaning if you leave, you can't practice within X miles for Y period). These have come under scrutiny and some states have limited them for physicians, but be aware of them and consider negotiating them if they're onerous. Another trend is the inclusion of value-based incentives (for quality metrics, patient satisfaction) in addition to volume metrics. While these might not heavily impact your first year, they indicate the shift in healthcare towards rewarding outcomes, not just output.

Retention and First Job Changes: It's an interesting fact that a significant number of physicians do not stay very long in their first job. Surveys have shown that around half of new physicians leave their first employer within 3-5 years. In one survey, only 37% planned to stay at their first job beyond their initial contract term. The main reasons for leaving included compensation, work-life balance, and management issues. This isn't to discourage you – but rather to highlight the importance of finding a good fit and also negotiating fairly upfront. It also means if your first job isn't perfect, you're not alone if you move on. Employers know this and that's why they work hard on physician engagement and retention strategies. As a new grad, try to discern during interviews if physicians there seem satisfied and if the organization is one that listens to feedback (you might even gently ask "What's the turnover like here?").

Work-Life Balance Priorities: Newer generations of physicians (millennials and Gen Z) have placed a higher emphasis on work-life balance. Many prioritize manageable call schedules, flexibility (part-time or specific hours), and supportive cultures. Employers are aware of this and some are offering creative schedules (e.g., 4-day workweeks, job-sharing, hybrid telemedicine days). If such things are important to you, know that you're part of a broader trend and it's okay to inquire about them once you have an offer in hand or are close to it. Early-career doctors often value location and lifestyle even above income – one survey noted work-life balance and location were top factors, with income secondary for many, especially women.

In summary, the job market for new attending physicians is robust, though your individual experience will depend on specialty and geography. Most new physicians have ample job choices, with recruiters and employers eager to sign them. The challenge is sorting through the options and finding the position that aligns with your goals. By knowing the general trends – like how jobs are found (networking!), how long it might take, and what to expect in contracts – you can navigate the process more effectively and land not just any job, but the right job for you.

Chapter 2

Personal Branding and Professional Reputation

Beyond clinical skills, your personal brand and professional reputation will shape how colleagues, employers, and patients perceive you. In this chapter, we'll explore how to deliberately cultivate a positive professional image both online and in person. The goal is not self-promotion for its own sake, but rather to communicate your values and strengths, and to avoid common pitfalls that could undermine trust. Let's dive into building your online presence, mastering real-world networking, defining your "clinical brand," and safeguarding your reputation.

2.1 Establishing Your Online Presence

In today's digital age, a physician's online presence is often the first touch-point for colleagues and patients. An up-to-date, professional profile on platforms like LinkedIn and Doximity can enhance your credibility. In fact, Doximity – a professional network just for healthcare – reports having over 80% of U.S. doctors as members, surpassing even the AMA in membership. Here's how to put your best foot forward online.

Create Complete Profiles: Don't settle for a bare-bones page. Fill out your education, training, specialty, skills, and contact information on LinkedIn and Doximity. A more complete profile ranks higher in searches and draws more engagement. Include relevant keywords (e.g. "cardiology fellow," "quality improvement") so that others can easily find you by specialty or interests.

Use a Professional Photo: First impressions count. Profiles with a photo are 21 times more likely to be viewed on LinkedIn. Use a clear, recent headshot in professional attire (white coat or business casual) against a neutral background. This helps convey trust and makes you recognizable when you meet contacts in real life.

Craft a Strong Headline and Summary: Instead of the default job title, write a headline that reflects your role and unique focus (e.g. "Internal Medicine Physician | Patient Educator and Diabetes Care Advocate"). In your bio summary, highlight your clinical interests, any research or leadership experience, and what you're passionate about as a physician. This is essentially your personal elevator pitch in written form.

Stay Active (Within Reason): Simply creating a profile isn't enough – try to log in periodically. Share a pertinent article you read, celebrate a milestone (like finishing board exams), or comment congratulating a colleague. Such activity keeps your profile visible. Joining professional groups on LinkedIn (for example, a group for your specialty or alumni of your residency) can foster connections. Aim for a professional tone in all posts – supportive, informative, and never controversial. Remember that even on "personal" social media, you are still a physician in the public eye.

On Doximity, after claiming your profile, you get useful tools like a free digital fax line and a public-facing profile that patients or other doctors might see. Ensure the information (clinic address, specialty, etc.) is accurate so that online physician directories (like U.S. News "Find a Doctor") have the right data. Just as with LinkedIn, profiles with photos on Doximity get preferential search ranking, so upload that professional headshot here as well.

A few additional tips for responsible social media use:

Separate Personal and Professional: It's wise to use privacy settings and even consider maintaining separate personal accounts. For example, you might keep a private Instagram for friends/family and a public LinkedIn or Twitter focused on professional content. Even so, assume anything you post could become public – privacy settings aren't foolproof.

Follow Guidelines and Ethics: The AMA Code of Medical Ethics advises being "cognizant of patient privacy and confidentiality... and refrain from posting identifiable patient information online." This means never share patient stories or images, even if anonymized (it's surprisingly easy for readers to guess the patient in a specific context). Also, maintain professional boundaries – for instance, it's usually not appropriate to "friend" your patients on social media.

Choose Platforms Wisely: If you're new to social media, LinkedIn and Doximity are great starting points for professional networking (What social media platform should doctors use first? - LinkedIn). Other platforms like Twitter (now X) or Instagram can be used professionally (many physicians share health tips or policy opinions), but proceed with caution and professionalism on those more casual channels. Everything you post contributes to your digital footprint and thus your reputation.

By establishing a thoughtful online presence, you make it easy for peers, mentors, or patients to learn about you in a positive way. Google yourself periodically to see what comes up – you want the top results to be your professional profiles or published work, not an old Facebook photo. In short, curate your online brand before someone else does it for you. It can open doors to opportunities and collaborations, while also reinforcing that you are a conscientious, modern physician.

2.2   In-Person Networking Essentials

Face-to-face interactions remain incredibly powerful in medicine. A chance meeting at a conference or a conversation at Grand Rounds can spark mentorships, job opportunities, or simply earn you a reputation as a collegial peer. As you start your first job, networking in person will help you integrate into the local medical community and beyond. Here's how to make those interactions count.

Be Prepared and Proactive at Conferences: Conferences and professional meetings are prime networking arenas. Don't just show up – plan ahead. If there are particular experts or potential mentors you'd like to meet, consider emailing them a couple of weeks in advance to ask if you could say hello during a break. A respectful, brief note introducing yourself and expressing interest in their work can set the stage: "Dear Dr. Smith, I enjoyed your recent article on heart failure management. I'll be at the Cardiology Conference next week and would love 5 minutes of your time after your panel, if possible." This approach is often more effective than hoping to catch them in a crowded hallway. Many seasoned physicians appreciate the initiative – they were in your shoes once and often are willing to chat with an early-career doc. At the conference, attend the social events and don't shy away from introducing yourself. Wear your name badge visibly and carry a few business cards if you have them. If you're nervous, remember a simple formula: introduce yourself with your name and institution, ask the other person about their work, and look for common ground. People love to talk about their own interests, so good questions are your secret weapon.

Make a Strong Impression in Hospital Meetings: Within your hospital or clinic, you'll have frequent encounters – department meetings, tumor boards, committee meetings, etc. Treat these as networking opportunities too. Arrive a few minutes early and greet people. Something as simple as, "Hi, I'm Dr. Patel, the new hire in internal medicine," with a smile and handshake can break the ice. Demonstrating enthusiasm and curiosity will help you stand out. You might say, "I'm excited to be here and get involved – any advice for a newbie?" This invites experienced staff to share and shows humility. Listening is key: in your first meetings, absorb the group dynamics and politics before asserting opinions. Over time, contributing thoughtful comments or questions will display that you're engaged. Also, reliability builds reputation: if you volunteer for a small task (say, helping to organize the next journal club), follow through diligently. Each positive interaction – no matter how small – spreads the message that you are a collegial and dependable physician.

Join Professional Organizations (and Actually Engage): Consider becoming a member of organizations relevant to your specialty or local area. National societies (like the American College of Physicians, American Academy of Pediatrics, etc.) offer conferences, committees, and online forums to meet peers. Many have sections or mentorship programs for young physicians. Local medical societies (county or state) are also valuable for connecting with physicians in your area across specialties. These groups provide ready-made communities that can support you. The benefits of active membership are numerous: networking with peers and industry experts, staying updated on best practices and policy changes, and finding mentors outside your workplace. For example, through a state medical society you might meet an older physician who can advise on career decisions, or through a specialty college you could join a committee that aligns with your interests (like a committee on health IT if you're tech-inclined). Simply joining isn't enough – you get out what you put in. Volunteer for a sub-committee or attend the mixers and educational events. Physicians who actively engage often find leadership opportunities and even job leads emerging from these connections. Moreover, participation in professional groups contributes to a sense of community and can counteract the isolation that sometimes contributes to burnout. Building these external networks also gives you a broader perspective on healthcare beyond your own workplace, which can spark new ideas and confidence.

Master Everyday Networking Etiquette: Remember that networking happens anywhere – in the doctors' lounge, elevator, or even the cafeteria line. Small gestures go a long way. Learn the names of nurses, techs, front-desk staff, and referring physicians you interact with. A friendly greeting in the morning, or a, "How's your day going?" shows that you value the whole team, not just those at your level. This isn't just being nice – a strong rapport with staff often leads to better teamwork and they'll be more inclined to have your back (like accommodating a last-minute patient or quickly facilitating a request) because they know and like you. If you're in a group practice, spend a few lunch breaks joining colleagues rather than eating alone; casual conversations can build camaraderie. You might discover shared hobbies or family connections that deepen professional friendships.

Which organizations should you join? If you have to be selective (memberships can be pricey), prioritize one in your specialty and one local general society. Specialty boards often offer discounted dues for early-career physicians and include subscriptions to journals or CME. Local societies connect you with community physicians and often involve advocacy (for example, coordinating with state legislators on healthcare issues). Evaluate what aligns with your goals: interested in research? Your specialty's research arm or a young investigator section could be worthwhile. Want leadership experience? A young physicians section of an association might be a place to volunteer. Over time, you can reassess membership value, but early on they are excellent avenues to find your tribe in the wider medical world.

In summary, in-person networking is about being intentional and approachable. Show up, be friendly, and show interest in others. Many opportunities in medicine still arise from word-of-mouth and personal connections. By expanding your network, you're not only opening doors for yourself but also building a support system of colleagues who can offer advice, referrals, or just camaraderie throughout your career.

2.3 Cultivating Your "Clinical Brand"

Beyond general professionalism, think about what distinguishes you as a physician. What do you want to be known for? It could be a clinical focus ("the new OB/GYN who is great with high-risk pregnancies"), a personal trait (like approachability or thoroughness), or a core value (such as commitment to patient education or health equity). Cultivating your "clinical brand" means identifying your unique strengths and interests – essentially, defining your professional identity – and consistently reflecting that in your work and communications.

What is a personal brand in medicine? It's not a logo or a sales gimmick; it's the combination of your expertise, values, and personality that you present to the world. One definition describes physician personal branding as "creating a professional identity that showcases your expertise, values, and unique approach to care," combining your clinical skills, reputation, and personality. In other words, it's the answer to "Tell me about yourself as a doctor" – the story that others remember about you.

Start by identifying your key strengths and passions. Reflect on what drew you to your specialty and what colleagues or mentors have praised about you. Maybe you have a talent for explaining complex medical issues in plain language, or a zeal for using technology to improve care, or a particular clinical niche (e.g. addiction medicine within family practice). These are clues to your brand. It can be helpful to write down a few descriptors or a sentence that encapsulates your approach. For example: "I'm Dr. Chen, a pediatrician who believes in partnering closely with parents on their child's health – I focus on preventive care and making medical information accessible." This clarity will guide how you present yourself in bios, during introductions, or on your website.

Next, align your actions and communication with that brand. Consistency builds recognition. If your brand is being an empathetic listener, make sure every patient interaction, every team meeting, reflects that – over time, people will say "She really listens." If your focus is a clinical niche, seek out ways to reinforce it: perhaps give a lunchtime talk on that topic, or become the go-to person in your practice for that issue. For instance, a young endocrinologist with a passion for diabetes technology might ensure they're up to date on the latest insulin pumps and volunteer to run a workshop for colleagues on that – soon, word gets around that "he's our diabetes tech expert."

Don't hesitate to showcase your expertise and interests – tactfully. In practice, this might mean:

- Offering to present at a case conference on a subject you have interest or background in (which highlights your knowledge).
- **Publishing or blogging:** If you enjoy writing, even a short piece on a reputable blog or a letter to the editor in a journal can start to get your name associated with that topic. Sharing your writings or thoughts on your LinkedIn (in a humble way) further solidifies your image as someone engaged with the field. Being a physician thought leader is not reserved for senior doctors; even early in your career, you can contribute. Consider that 26% of doctors said personal branding positively impacted their career opportunities and patient care in a recent survey. Opportunities like speaking at community events, being contacted by media for comments, or being invited to collaborate often arise because people know what you're about.
- **Engaging online carefully:** If building an online presence beyond LinkedIn – such as a professional Twitter account or a personal website – align it to your brand. For example, a rehab medicine physician who's passionate about fitness might share exercise tips or rehab success stories (with patient permission) on a blog. One case study is Dr. Kevin Pho (KevinMD), who built a huge following and is seen as a leading voice in physician social media; he established his brand around giving physicians a voice and discussing current issues, garnering over 3 million monthly blog views. Now, you don't need millions of followers, but the principle is to be known for something positive.

Importantly, your clinical brand should be genuine, not an act. Patients and colleagues can sense insincerity. Authenticity in branding builds trust. For example, if you naturally have a warm, informal style with patients, that is your brand – embrace it and don't feel pressure to adopt a stiff persona just because you're now an attending. Conversely, if you're more introverted and methodical, you might brand yourself around thoroughness and evidence-based practice. Authenticity also means vulnerability – acknowledging what you don't know and showing you're always learning. This humanizes you. As one physician put it, "the best marketing is a good clinical and humanized practice" – meaning that genuinely caring for patients and treating them well ultimately speaks louder than any branding campaign.

It helps to have a succinct introduction of your professional self. You will be meeting a lot of new people. Having a 1-2 line self-introduction that highlights your unique angle can leave a memorable impression. For example: "I'm Dr. Lopez, I just joined the cardiology team. I have a particular interest in sports cardiology since I was an athlete before med school, so I love helping active people stay heart-healthy." This shares a bit of personal passion (sports) and professional focus (sports cardiology), distinguishing Dr. Lopez from a generic "new cardiologist." The person you meet might later think, "Oh right, she's the cardiologist who works with athletes."

If part of your brand is a value (e.g. compassion, integrity, innovation), look for ways to demonstrate it. The physician known for community service might organize a free clinic day. The doctor known for innovation might pilot a new telehealth tool at the practice. Early in your career, you have the fresh energy to undertake such initiatives – doing so not only is rewarding but cements your reputation in that light.

Finally, remember that branding is also about legacy and long-term vision. It's okay if you're not 100% sure what niche you want to occupy; your brand can evolve. Early on, focus on a couple of strengths and interests, and cultivate those. As you grow, your brand might sharpen (you might discover a passion for teaching and become "that doctor who's a fantastic teacher," or you might delve into research and become known for that). Think of your brand as your professional reputation by design – it's the answer to "What sets you apart from the physician in the next office?" A clear clinical brand not only differentiates you but can also guide your career choices, ensuring you pursue opportunities aligned with your identity. It makes it easier for mentors and sponsors to think of you when specific opportunities arise ("We need someone to head a new diabetes program – what about that new doc who's really into diabetes care?").

2.4   Protecting Your Reputation

A hard-earned reputation can be tarnished in moments. As a new physician, you must be vigilant against missteps that can damage trust with patients, colleagues, or the public. This section covers common pitfalls – especially in our digital era – and how to avoid them, so that your professional image remains as strong as your clinical skills.

Social Media and Online Caution: One of the biggest modern threats to a physician's reputation is careless use of social media. Posts that might seem benign can violate ethical or legal standards. An important rule: **never post any patient-identifiable information, ever, even in closed groups. There have been multiple cases of clinicians facing HIPAA violations for social media posts**. Notably, posting "verbal gossip" about a patient, even without names, is considered a HIPAA violation. For example, a nurse was fired after venting in a Facebook post about a patient (not naming them, but giving context that made it easy to figure out). In another case, a doctor posted a selfie with an unconscious patient in the background – a clear breach of privacy. The HIPAA law defines 18 specific identifiers (like age, dates, geographic details, etc.) that could identify a patient. It's surprisingly easy for a reader to put two and two together, especially in small communities where "65-year-old man with a new hip" describes only one person in town. The safest practice is: never discuss patient cases on social media at all, even if anonymized. If you want to share a general lesson or story, change every possible detail and still get permission if applicable. Better yet, share through professional channels like case reports or de-identified teaching platforms, rather than public social media.

The digital permanence of online content is another concern. Deleting a tweet or post doesn't guarantee it's gone; screenshots live forever. Thus, avoid impulsive posts especially on contentious topics. As the AMA Code of Ethics warns, "once on the internet, content is likely there permanently," and actions online "may negatively affect [physicians'] reputations among patients and colleagues". Before posting, consider the "front page test": would you be comfortable if your post was on the front page of tomorrow's newspaper, with your name next to it? If not, don't post it. This applies to more than patient info – it includes bad-mouthing your workplace, colleagues, or making off-color jokes. There have been infamous instances of doctors whose tweets with derogatory remarks or privacy breaches led to job loss and public shaming. Even in private messaging or closed groups, be cautious; things can leak.

Responsible Social Media Use: Does this mean you can't use social media at all? Not necessarily – many physicians use it constructively (for advocacy, education, or community). But follow best practices: keep your personal life settings private and separate from any public professional profile. Don't accept friend requests from current patients on your personal accounts; if you use a professional page, keep interactions general and professional (no individual medical advice online!). Avoid discussing your workday in detail – for instance, "Tough day, lost a patient in surgery" might seem okay since it's anonymous, but it could be sensitive if family or staff see it. Also, be mindful of photos – a selfie at work could accidentally include a patient's name on a chart behind you, which is a HIPAA violation.

One clinic manager posted a harmless office party photo on Instagram not noticing patient files in the background – that led to reprimand. Always double-check images for any patient info.

Furthermore, if you see a colleague posting something unprofessional, consider intervening politely or alerting appropriate channels. The AMA advises that physicians have a responsibility to help maintain standards online – if a peer's post is inappropriate, ideally speak to them to take it down, and if it's egregious and they don't, report it. This isn't tattling; it's protecting patient privacy and the profession's integrity.

Reputation protection isn't just online. In day-to-day practice, certain behaviors can erode trust quickly. A few things to guard against:

HIPAA and Privacy in Practice: We've covered online privacy, but be mindful in the hospital too. Hallway conversations carry. Don't discuss patients in the elevator or cafeteria where others can overhear (it sounds obvious, but in a rushed day, people slip up). Always log off or lock screens when stepping away from a workstation to prevent unauthorized access to records. These habits signal to staff that you take confidentiality seriously, further bolstering your reputation for integrity.

Respectful Communication: How you treat others – especially those who have less institutional power than you – speaks volumes. Yelling at a nurse or demeaning a medical assistant is a surefire way to become infamous for the wrong reasons. News of unprofessional outbursts spreads quickly in a workplace. If you feel frustration rising (for example, a consult wasn't called, or a lab test was mishandled), take a breather and address it in a calm, private manner. Being the doctor who stays calm under stress and treats everyone with respect will earn you admiration from the team. This also extends to how you talk about others. Avoid gossip or joining in on negative talk about colleagues. It's easy to bond over shared gripes, but it can backfire. If someone constantly bad-mouths others to you, you can imagine they might bad-mouth you to others as well. Maintain a reputation as someone who stays above petty politics.

Honesty and Ethics: Early in your practice you'll encounter situations testing your ethical compass. Always choose the ethical path, even if it's harder. That could be disclosing an error openly rather than trying to cover it up, or admitting "I don't know, but I will find out" to a patient instead of bluffing. Honesty builds trust. Cutting corners with documentation or billing, even if "everyone does it," can end your career if discovered. Remember, physicians are held to high standards – things like DUI arrests, fraud, or improper relationships will not only ruin your reputation but can cost you your license. While it sounds extreme, many careers have been derailed by lapses in judgment outside of clinical medicine. Keep your personal life clean and professional life transparent.

Social Events: As you join a new team, there may be informal socials: dinners, happy hours, holiday parties. These are great for camaraderie, but be mindful that even in social settings you are still with work colleagues. Over-imbibing and doing something inappropriate at a work party will become legend by Monday (not the legend you want to be). Enjoy yourself, but set a personal limit on alcohol and avoid divisive topics. It should go without saying, but romantic advances toward coworkers or staff in these settings can also create reputational and legal issues (especially if there is any power differential). In short, professional boundaries apply after hours too.

Learn from Others' Mistakes: It's helpful to read about physicians who faced disciplinary action for professionalism lapses – many state boards publish anonymized cases. Common themes include: mishandling patient information, inappropriate social media posts, boundary violations with patients (e.g., online interactions that became too personal), and unprofessional public behavior. The takeaway is that one moment of poor judgment can undo years of hard work. But by being aware of these risks, you're already a step ahead in avoiding them.

Mistakes may still happen. We're all human. Despite precautions, you might slip – maybe you tweet something that gets backlash, or you lose your temper once in a tense moment. How you respond is crucial. Take accountability immediately. If it's an online misstep, delete the post and apologize if appropriate (but avoid a defensive fight online). If it's internal (like you snapped at a nurse), seek them out to sincerely apologize and explain the stressor without making excuses. Often a genuine apology and effort to do better will contain the damage. Proactively inform your supervisor if it's something that might reach them; it's better they hear it from you with context than from someone else. Demonstrating insight and remorse can actually strengthen your colleagues' respect for you in the long run, because it shows professionalism and maturity.

Above all, protecting your reputation boils down to maintaining professionalism, confidentiality, and respect in all settings. Think of your reputation as part of patient care – if patients and staff trust you, they will work with you more effectively, leading to better outcomes. It takes time to build that trust capital, but only an instant to lose it. By being mindful of your actions and the potential consequences, you'll keep that capital intact and growing. Your good name is one of your greatest assets as a physician – nurture it carefully.

Chapter 3

Understanding Physician Practice Models

One of the biggest decisions you'll face is choosing where and how to practice medicine. There are many types of practice models – from hanging out your own shingle in solo practice to joining a large health system or exploring telemedicine. Each option has its own culture, expectations, and trade-offs. The "right" choice depends on your personal priorities and career goals. It helps to understand what each model looks like in terms of day-to-day work, level of independence, typical patient mix, and opportunities for growth. In recent years, there's been a trend toward physicians becoming employees (rather than practice owners) – in fact, most U.S. patient-care physicians now work outside of doctor-owned practices. However, every model remains viable, and the best fit is the one that aligns with your needs and desires. Let's explore the common practice settings, with some seasoned advice on the pros, cons, and key considerations of each.

3.1 Solo Private Practice

Solo practice means you are the only physician in your practice – essentially running your own small medical business. You have no partners and no affiliation with a larger organization. Typically, you'll have a small staff (perhaps a nurse, medical assistant, and office manager) and a relatively limited patient base. In this model, you're in charge of everything: from clinical care to administrative tasks like hiring staff, managing billing, and negotiating with insurers. It's like being the CEO and the primary worker of your clinic.

Pros

Maximum Autonomy: You have ultimate control over how you practice medicine. Being the owner gives you "the utmost autonomy to practice the way you want", from setting clinic policies to deciding how much time to spend with each patient.

Personalized Patient Care: With a smaller patient panel, you can build close, one-on-one relationships. Many solo practitioners enjoy knowing their patients deeply and providing a personal touch in care. You can shape the practice to reflect your values and style of medicine.

Independence in Operations: Because you're in charge, you can design your office workflow, choose your electronic records system, and make business decisions without needing consensus from partners. This freedom can be very rewarding for entrepreneurial physicians.

Cons

All Responsibilities on You: While this option offers the most freedom, it can also be the most difficult. Running a solo practice means all the administrative and business burdens fall on your shoulders – hiring and managing staff, dealing with billing and insurance paperwork, compliance with regulations, etc. There's no larger entity handling these tasks for you.

Long or Unpredictable Hours: Because you are the only doctor, you may have to handle patient needs at all hours. If a patient calls after hours or a crisis occurs on the weekend, you're the one on call. Taking vacation can be tricky – you'll need to arrange coverage or risk pausing your practice. It's not uncommon for solo docs to have "unpredictable work hours" while they juggle clinical care and practice management.

Financial and Logistic Challenges: Solo practitioners face high start-up costs and overhead. You must pay for office space, equipment, malpractice insurance, salaries, etc., all on your own. There's also the challenge of attracting enough patients to sustain the practice. In the beginning, building a patient base requires time and marketing, especially if you're new to the community . This model can carry more financial risk and stress compared to a salaried job, especially early on.

Solo practice offers the highest autonomy – you make all decisions about care and operations. The schedule can be very demanding; while you can set office hours to your liking, you're also the one covering nights/weekends unless you arrange cross-coverage with other physicians. Your patient mix might be broad (especially in primary care) but limited to those you personally recruit – often allowing deeper continuity with families over time. In terms of career development, solo practice doesn't usually include formal teaching or research, but it does develop your skills as a leader and business owner. You might become a respected community physician and can pursue leadership in local medical societies or hospital staff, but you won't have the structured academic promotions that come with university settings.

3.2   Group Private Practice

In a group practice, you join forces with other physicians in a shared practice setting. This may be a single-specialty group (e.g., an internal medicine group) or a multispecialty group with different types of doctors under one organization. Some groups are partnerships where senior physicians are owners and junior physicians can become partners over time, while others might structure physicians as employees of the group. The key feature is that resources and responsibilities are shared. You'll work alongside colleagues, sharing office space, staff, and equipment, and often collaborating on patient care.

Pros

Shared Workload and Coverage: In a well-run group, you have teammates to share patient care duties. This means you can arrange coverage for evenings or weekends – the burden of being on call is spread across multiple providers, allowing more flexibility in scheduling than in solo practice. For example, if the practice has four physicians, each might take call only every 4th weekend. This can lead to a more predictable work schedule.

Resource Sharing: Group practices benefit from economies of scale. With multiple doctors, it's easier to afford a robust office staff and potentially better equipment or an electronic medical record system. Administrative tasks and overhead costs are shared, so each individual physician carries less of the business burden than a solo doc. For instance, the practice might have a dedicated billing specialist or office manager handling day-to-day operations for all physicians.

Established Patient Base: If you join an existing group, you often gain access to an established patient base. Your colleagues might already have a referral network and a reputation in the community, which can jumpstart your own patient panel. This can mean steadier workflow and less uncertainty when you're starting out.

Collegial Support: There's inherent value in having peers next door. You can easily bounce cases off colleagues, get quick curbside consults, and learn from each other's experiences. For new attendings, this mentorship and collaboration can ease the transition into practice. It can also foster a sense of camaraderie and reduce the professional isolation that some solo practitioners experience.

Cons

Reduced Autonomy: Decision-making is shared, so you won't have complete control the way you would solo. Your autonomy is limited when you have partners – meaning that group decisions (like scheduling, hiring, investments in new equipment, or even the style of patient care) may not always align perfectly with your personal preferences. You'll need to compromise at times.

Governance and Conflict Resolution: Working closely with partners means differences of opinion will arise. Whether it's how to divide income, whether to expand the office, or how to manage a difficult employee, group practices require negotiation and consensus. This can sometimes slow down decision-making or create friction if not well-managed. New physicians especially might have "less of a voice" in major practice decisions initially, depending on the group's structure (for example, non-partner physicians may have limited say until they become partners).

Shared Financial Risk (and Reward): While costs and risks are shared (a pro), it also means the financial outcomes (good or bad) are distributed. If one physician in the group underperforms or racks up expenses, it can affect everyone. Also, joining a group as a new partner often involves "buying in" to the practice – essentially purchasing a share – which can be a significant upfront investment. The price and terms for partnership vary, and until you're an owner, you might be an employee with a pathway to partnership.

A group practice offers moderate autonomy – you have independence in your own patient care, but collective decisions will govern the practice's operations. The schedule tends to be more predictable and balanced; you can take time off knowing colleagues can cover, though you'll also cover for them in turn. The patient mix might expand compared to solo – for instance, a multispecialty group can internally refer patients to each other, so you might see cases that your partners send you and vice versa, broadening the scope. You'll also inherit some longstanding patients from an established practice. For career development, group practice can offer leadership roles (e.g., managing partner, head of a department within the group) and the chance to learn business skills in a collaborative setting. There's no formal academic advancement, but you can still engage in continuing education, possibly group-led quality improvement projects, or community health initiatives as a team.

3.3 Hospital Employment

Hospital employment means you work directly for a hospital (or hospital-owned clinic) as a salaried or contracted physician. The hospital (or the health system owning the hospital) is your employer. Physicians in virtually all specialties can be hospital-employed – from internists and hospitalists, to surgeons, anesthesiologists, emergency physicians, and even outpatient specialists if the hospital system owns clinics. In this model, the institution handles most administrative aspects of practice. You practice medicine, and the hospital takes care of staff hiring, billing, facility management, and so on. Physicians may work on inpatient units, in the emergency department, or in hospital-operated outpatient centers.

Pros

Focus on Patient Care: Without the need to run a business, you can devote more of your time and energy to clinical duties. Employed physicians don't have to worry about managing billing staff or negotiating office leases – the hospital administration handles those operational concerns. This often means more time for patients or personal life compared to private owners who must split time with business tasks.

Team and Resource Support: Hospitals provide a robust support infrastructure. You typically have access to a broad range of resources and technology – for example, on-site labs, imaging, specialists for consults, and advanced medical equipment. There's also backup if emergencies arise: in a hospital setting, you work within a team of nurses, allied health professionals, and other doctors, which can make delivering care more efficient. Additionally, the hospital usually handles administrative support (scheduling patients, coding/billing, ensuring compliance), so those burdens are lifted from you.

Structured Schedule (Potentially Predictable): Many hospital-employed roles come with set shifts or clinic hours. For example, as a hospitalist you might work 7-on/7-off shifts, or as an emergency physician you'll have scheduled shifts. This can translate to a more predictable schedule and work-life separation. Depending on the department's needs, you might have more regular hours than in a small private practice. When you're off duty, typically another colleague or on-call service covers patient needs, meaning your free time is truly free (especially in shift-based roles).

Stability and Less Financial Risk: The hospital assumes the business risk. You draw a salary (or other agreed compensation, though we won't delve into pay structures here) and typically receive benefits like health insurance and malpractice coverage through the employer. This model can feel more secure for those who don't want to worry about the fluctuations of running a practice.

Cons

Less Autonomy: As a hospital-employed physician, you must adhere to hospital policies and protocols. There will be guidelines on how to practice (e.g., care pathways, formularies for medications you can prescribe) and possibly productivity or quality targets you're expected to meet. Clinical decisions might occasionally be influenced by institutional rules – for example, referral restrictions or required pre-authorizations for certain tests. In short, you trade some independence for the support the hospital provides.

Bureaucracy and Administration: Large institutions can be bureaucratic. Changes to how the clinic or unit operates may require approval from multiple committees, which can be frustrating if you're used to making quick decisions. Employed doctors often have to attend meetings or participate in hospital committees (quality improvement, compliance, etc.) as part of their duties. This "red tape" can sometimes slow down innovations or adjustments you'd like to implement.

Less Continuity with Patients: Depending on your role, you might have less long-term relationship with patients. For example, hospitalists and ER doctors see patients for short episodes and then hand off care. Even outpatient physicians employed by a hospital might find that patients get rotated or referred within the system. Continuity of care can be less than in private practice, where patients usually identify with a specific personal doctor. If deep ongoing patient relationships are important to you, consider how the role structures follow-ups and referrals.

Scheduling Rigidity: While the schedule can be predictable, it can also be inflexible. Vacation time, for instance, might need to be requested far in advance and is subject to departmental staffing needs. You may work some nights, weekends, or holidays as required by the hospital rotation, which is an expected part of the job rather than something you can opt out of.

In a hospital-employed model, physician autonomy is often lower than in private practice – you operate within an organizational framework and answer to administrative leadership. The schedule is stable in the sense of defined shifts/hours, but you have to fit into the hospital's staffing plan (which might involve night shifts or holiday coverage in some fields). The patient mix in hospitals is usually more acute – you'll treat inpatients with serious illnesses or see higher acuity cases in the ED, for example. If you're in a hospital-owned outpatient clinic, your patient mix might be similar to private practice, but with more referrals from within the system and possibly a higher volume demand. Career development in hospital employment can take the form of administrative pathways (you might become a medical director, department chief, or head of quality improvement) since large systems often promote physicians into leadership. There may also be institutional support for continuing education. However, if academic teaching or research is your goal, a pure hospital job may not provide that, unless it's an academic hospital (in which case, see academic medicine below).

3.4 Large Healthcare System / HMO Employment

This category is related to hospital employment, but on a broader scale. Large healthcare systems (for example, Kaiser Permanente, the Veterans Health Administration, or big multi-hospital networks) employ physicians across multiple facilities and clinics. Often, these are integrated systems or Health Maintenance Organizations (HMOs) where the focus is on providing coordinated care within one network. In such models, the organization might have its own hospitals, outpatient centers, and even insurance plan. Physicians are employees of the system, which emphasizes standardization and cost-effective care across the network. You might work in a clinic or hospital owned by the system, and your patients generally use that network for all their care.

Pros

Work-Life Balance and Predictable Hours: Large systems tend to have structured schedules for physicians, often aiming for clinician work-life balance to prevent burnout. For example, an HMO clinic job might be 8–5 with set patient slots and minimal after-hours duty. Physicians in these settings often report having more regular and predictable work hours, which can be a big plus if you value consistency.

Extensive Administrative Support: Similar to hospital employment, big systems handle the administrative side for you – credentialing, billing, patient scheduling, compliance, all are taken care of by the organization. This allows you to focus on seeing patients. Large healthcare organizations often have robust IT systems, call centers, care coordinators, and other supports that reduce your non-clinical workload.

Resources and Stability: Being part of a large network means you have access to extensive resources. There may be internal referral networks, system-wide protocols for best practices, and teams for population health management. You also typically enjoy job stability; big systems don't usually disappear overnight. In fact, this model is considered one of the least financially risky from a physician standpoint (since the system absorbs financial ups and downs).

Coordinated Patient Care: In an integrated system/HMO, patient care is designed to be seamless and coordinated. All your patients' records are within one system, making communication with other specialists easy. For physicians who like teamwork and holistic care, this can be rewarding – you're part of a large care team aiming for consistent quality.

Cons

Less Clinical Autonomy: Large systems often have strict guidelines and formularies. Independent decision-making can be limited by organizational policies aimed at cost control and standardization. For instance, you might need to follow specific treatment algorithms or get approvals for tests that would be automatic in private practice. Some doctors feel creativity or personalized approaches are constrained in this environment.

Bureaucracy and Pace of Change: The bigger the system, the more layers of management. If you have an idea to improve a clinic process or want to acquire new equipment, you'll likely need to go through multiple committees or budget approvals. This can be slow and occasionally frustrating. Innovation may take longer to implement than in a nimble private office.

Patient Volume and Protocols: To meet system-wide targets, you may be expected to see a high volume of patients or adhere to time limits per visit. Large HMOs focus on efficiency; while they value quality, you might feel pressure to keep patient visits short and stick to checklists. Also, because patients pay into a network, they might have limited choices, and you could encounter patients dissatisfied with system rules (for example, needing referrals for everything). Dealing with those frustrations can be part of the job.

Geographical and Organizational Hierarchy: In large systems, decisions might be made by people far removed from your local practice (headquarters in another state, for example). This can lead to physicians feeling like "cogs in a machine." Additionally, you might be one physician among hundreds or thousands in the organization, so distinguishing yourself for promotions or new opportunities might require extra initiative.

Autonomy in large system employment is generally low – you follow the system's care models and policies closely. The schedule is often quite favorable (regular hours, protected time off, coverage for leave) which can improve work-life integration. The patient mix depends on the system's population; many HMOs emphasize primary care and preventive services, so if you're a specialist, you'll see patients within that referral network. The patient population could be very diverse (e.g., an HMO serving a wide community) but also somewhat closed network (patients typically only see providers within the system). Career development can include moving into management or quality roles in the organization. Large systems often have leadership training for physicians and pathways to become a department chief or regional medical director. If research interests you, some systems (like large academic-affiliated networks or the VA) support clinical research or pilot programs, but pure private HMOs might offer less academic activity.

3.5 Academic Medicine (Teaching Hospitals and Universities)

Academic medicine refers to working for a medical school, teaching hospital, or university health system where your role includes patient care and academic duties. As an academic physician (e.g., faculty at a university hospital), you'll likely wear several hats: clinician, teacher, and possibly researcher. Teaching medical students and residents is a core part of the job, and you might supervise trainees on rounds or in clinic. There's also an expectation to engage in scholarly work – which could range from research and publishing to quality improvement projects or educational scholarship. Academics often practice in large tertiary-care centers that see complex cases and referrals from the region.

Pros

Intellectual Stimulation & Cutting-Edge Medicine: Academic centers are at "the cutting edge of knowledge and skills," often tackling patients with rare or challenging conditions. If you love learning, academics keeps you constantly stimulated – you're surrounded by colleagues who are experts in their fields, grand rounds and lectures are frequent, and you have opportunities to participate in research that advances medicine.

Teaching and Mentorship: Many physicians find it deeply rewarding to teach the next generation of doctors. In academia, a portion of your time is dedicated to educating medical students, residents, or fellows. Guiding young doctors and seeing them grow can be a source of professional pride and personal satisfaction. It also keeps you on your toes – trainees ask insightful questions and challenge you to stay updated.

Opportunities for New Roles: Academic institutions offer many paths for career development. Besides climbing the faculty ladder (from Assistant to Associate to full Professor), you can take on roles like residency Program Director, clerkship director, research lab head, or serve on academic committees. There are also plenty of conferences and collaboration opportunities. If you have a passion (be it global health, ethics, simulation training, etc.), academia often has outlets for it.

Collaborative Environment and Prestige: Being part of a renowned university or teaching hospital can carry a certain prestige and open doors to collaborate with top people in your specialty. Academics fosters a culture of continual improvement and inquiry. Additionally, academic jobs often come with robust benefits and time off for conferences or study (for example, many universities have generous vacation plus allotted days for academic travel or coursework).

Cons

Lower Clinical Autonomy (and Bureaucracy): Although you have freedom in clinical decision-making, you still must abide by hospital rules and training requirements. Sometimes the needs of the residency program or students (like teaching rounds, paperwork for evaluations) can intrude on clinical efficiency. Also, universities are known for committees – decisions often require multiple meetings and approvals. Bureaucracy in academia can be significant, from grant administration to IRB approvals for research, to paperwork for academic promotions.

Balancing Multiple Responsibilities: Perhaps the biggest challenge is juggling the "triad" of clinical care, teaching, and research. Your day might include seeing patients in the morning, lecturing at noon, and working on a research paper in the afternoon. It can feel like having multiple jobs in one, and time management is critical. You might find yourself coming in early or staying late to catch up on research or grading papers after your clinical work is done. This balancing act can be stressful and sometimes leads to working beyond the typical hours (even if the base schedule seems lighter).

Service Obligations and Workload: Academic physicians often have to fill in gaps that trainees can't cover. For instance, when residents are restricted by duty hour limits, attending physicians step in to ensure patient care is continuous – faculty may end up filling patient-care gaps when residents are off duty. Teaching hospitals can be understaffed relative to patient needs, relying on faculty to shoulder extra clinical load at times. Moreover, the documentation for teaching (like supervising notes, signing off on trainee orders, etc.) adds to the clinical workload.

Compensation Considerations: Academic positions traditionally pay less than private sector jobs, and budgets at teaching hospitals (often safety-net hospitals) can be tight. This can translate to fewer resources for your department or limitations on how fast the institution can grow your program. Financially, you might have to supplement your income with grants or extra work if that's important to you. (On the flip side, as mentioned, benefits like retirement plans and tuition discounts for family can be advantages in academia, but these are ancillary to our focus on practice structure.)

Autonomy in academic medicine is a mixed bag – you have a lot of intellectual freedom to pursue research or innovative care models, but day-to-day clinical autonomy might be moderated by teaching requirements and department policies. The schedule can be very segmented: you might have certain days for clinic, certain weeks for inpatient service, and others for research or teaching. This variety is stimulating but also means your routine is less steady week to week. You'll likely have built-in time for non-clinical duties (e.g., one day a week for research), which is a perk if used well. The patient mix is often highly complex and specialized: academic centers get referrals of rare cases and very ill patients, providing a rich learning experience. You'll also see a steady flow of patients who come specifically because it's a teaching hospital or tertiary center. Continuity may suffer if teams rotate, but you often manage a panel in outpatient settings and follow some inpatients long-term through specialty clinics. In terms of career development, academic medicine provides a formal ladder and titles, as well as chances to gain recognition in your field (through research publications, presenting at conferences, etc.). It's the route if you aspire to be a nationally known expert or department chair someday. Conversely, if you're not interested in scholarly work, the additional duties in academia might feel like a burden – some physicians opt out of academics for this reason after a few years.

3.6   Locum Tenens

Locum tenens is Latin for "one holding a place" – essentially, a temporary physician who fills in for others. As a locum tenens doctor, you typically work as an independent contractor on short-term assignments in various locations. For example, a hospital in a rural area might hire a locum tenens physician to cover for a doctor on leave, or a clinic might use locums until a permanent hire starts. These assignments can range from a few weeks to several months, and you might find them through agencies that specialize in locum placements. Locums work in all settings: hospitals, clinics, ERs, even internationally, depending on demand. You generally won't be a long-term member of any one medical staff, but rather a rotating professional stepping in where needed.

Pros

Flexibility and Freedom: Locum tenens offers perhaps the greatest flexibility of any practice model. "These positions offer flexibility regarding work schedules and locations". You can choose when and where to work – taking an assignment for a few months, then taking time off or moving to another location. This can be ideal if you want to travel, if you're unsure where you want to settle long-term, or if you have life circumstances (like a spouse in training in different cities) that make a permanent job less practical initially. You essentially set your own calendar by accepting assignments that fit your timing.

Variety of Experience: As a locum, you'll experience different medical environments and patient populations. One month you might be working at a small community hospital, the next at a large urban medical center, or in different regions of the country. This variety can rapidly broaden your clinical skills and adaptability. It's a bit like test-driving various practice settings – you get to see how different systems operate, which can inform what you ultimately want in a permanent job. For a new attending, locums can be a way to explore options before committing.

Minimal Administrative Hassles (per assignment): When you're on a locum assignment, you typically focus just on patient care; the facility that hires you will have its own staff and processes. You're not involved in the politics or administration long-term. Once your stint is done, you move on with no lingering duties. Also, many locum contracts cover your malpractice insurance and travel housing while on assignment, so those logistics are taken care of by the agency or employer.

Potential to Tailor Your Career: Some physicians make a full career out of locum work, enjoying the freedom it provides. Others use locums periodically (for example, doing a few weeks of locums each year in addition to a regular job, or working locums during a job transition or before retirement). It can be a versatile tool to craft a career that isn't confined to one location or employer.

Cons

Lack of Stability and Benefits: By nature, locum tenens positions are temporary and thus less stable. You might have a gap between assignments unless you plan well. There's also typically no benefits package – as an independent contractor you usually won't get health insurance, retirement plans, paid time off, etc., from the places you work. You'll need to budget for your own benefits and ensure you have personal health insurance, disability insurance, and so forth. The financial side requires planning (though we're not delving into compensation details here, note that locums often are paid well per unit time but with trade-offs like covering your own benefits).

Frequent Transitions: Being the "new doctor" repeatedly has challenges. With each new assignment, you have to learn a new electronic health record system, new hospital layout or clinic workflow, and build rapport quickly with staff. This constant adjustment can be tiring. You also might get the less desirable shifts (since you're filling in gaps) and have to prove yourself each place you go. If you value a consistent team and long-term relationships at work, locums will feel jarring.

Travel and Licensure Hassles: Locum work often involves travel, which can be a pro for adventure but a con for logistics. Living out of a suitcase or hotel for weeks can wear on you. Additionally, working in different states means you must obtain multiple state medical licenses and hospital privileges. The credentialing process at each institution can be cumbersome and time-consuming, sometimes taking months. Many locum agencies assist with this, but it's still paperwork and coordination you must stay on top of.

Limited Continuity and Connection: In locums, you usually don't have long-term follow-up with patients. You swoop in, treat patients, and then hand off to permanent staff when you leave. For some, this lack of ongoing patient relationships or project follow-through is unsatisfying. Similarly, while you'll meet many people, you might miss out on deeper collegial friendships that come with working in one place over time. You're not around for office parties, long-term quality improvement work, or seeing outcomes of changes implemented. In essence, you might sometimes feel like an outsider or a "substitute teacher" in each new workplace.

Autonomy in locum tenens can feel high in that you choose your assignments and aren't tied down; clinically, however, you must adapt to each facility's rules quickly – you have no say in hospital policies or workflows as a temp. The schedule is whatever you make it: you could work intense back-to-back assignments or space them out to enjoy long breaks (great for work-life balance if managed well). But day-to-day on assignment, you must fit the schedule they need – possibly irregular or heavy shifts – and be prepared for last-minute calls if you offer availability. The patient mix will vary widely with each job – one assignment might have you seeing rural underserved patients with a broad range of issues, another might be sub-specialized. This is enriching but also means you have to quickly acclimate to the community's health needs. Career development in the traditional sense (titles, promotions) doesn't really apply in locum work – you won't become "Chief of X" as a locum. However, you will develop incredible adaptability and breadth of experience. Some physicians use locums to network – for example, a successful locum stint can sometimes turn into a permanent job offer if you find a place you love. Keep in mind that doing locums early career can leave a gap in your CV in terms of steady positions, but it also can show you've practiced in various settings. It's a unique path that can be short-term or a lifestyle in itself.

3.7 Concierge Medicine / Direct Primary Care

Concierge medicine and Direct Primary Care (DPC) are practice models where physicians contract directly with patients for a membership or retainer fee, rather than billing traditional insurance for each visit. In a Direct Primary Care practice, patients typically pay a flat monthly or annual fee (e.g. $50–$100/month) that covers most primary care services. In a concierge practice, the fee is usually higher (sometimes several thousand dollars per year) and often aimed at more extensive "VIP" services – such as 24/7 physician availability, comprehensive annual wellness exams, and a very low physician-to-patient ratio. Both models drastically limit the number of patients per physician (often a few hundred instead of a few thousand in a typical practice) so that doctors can provide more personalized and accessible care. Concierge practices sometimes still bill insurance for visits in addition to the retainer, whereas pure DPC generally avoids insurance entirely. Many concierge/DPC practices are primary care, but there are concierge specialists too. These models can be set up as solo or small group practices.

Pros

Extremely High Autonomy: Because you contract directly with patients and usually have no insurance company dictating terms, you can practice medicine the way you think is best. You set the membership structure and the services included. There's significant freedom from insurance paperwork and approval hoops, which greatly cuts down administrative burden. This often means more time focusing on patient care rather than billing codes.

More Time with Patients: With a smaller patient panel, you can afford to spend 30 minutes, an hour, or even longer for appointments as needed. You're not forced into seeing 25 patients a day. Physicians in concierge/DPC often advertise same-day appointments that aren't rushed. This enhanced doctor-patient relationship is a major draw – you get to know your patients extremely well, and they feel taken care of. For the physician, it can bring back the feeling of old-fashioned personalized medicine, which can be very professionally fulfilling.

Flexible Schedule and Workload: Since you determine how many patients to take on, you effectively control your workload. If you want a lighter schedule, you can cap membership accordingly (recognizing that lower patient numbers must be balanced by charging a feasible fee). Many concierge physicians report less stress and a more enjoyable pace: seeing fewer patients leads to "less stress" and more focus on wellness of those patients. You can also often set aside time for house calls, wellness planning, or other services that traditional practices struggle to accommodate.

Patient Satisfaction: Patients who choose these models are typically very appreciative of the access and time they get. They often have your cell phone and can reach you with urgent needs any time. Knowing you're providing a high level of service and seeing patient satisfaction can be a big morale boost. It's gratifying to practice in a way where patients feel valued and heard – and it can remind you why you went into medicine in the first place.

Cons

Limited Patient Access / Ethical Concerns: Because of the membership fees, not everyone can afford this model. There's an ethical consideration: concierge medicine, in particular, tends to cater to wealthier or insured populations, potentially widening gaps in care. Some doctors feel uneasy limiting their practice to those who can pay a premium. If you pursue this, you might grapple with questions about how to ensure care for patients who can't join, or how your practice fits into the community's healthcare needs.

Business Risk and Patient Retention: In DPC/concierge, your income (and practice viability) depends on maintaining a certain number of subscribed patients. There's a dependence on patient enrollment stability. If many patients lose jobs (and thus discretionary income) or move away, your practice could suffer quickly. Marketing and continuously demonstrating your value (so people feel the membership is "worth it") are ongoing tasks. Especially early on, recruiting enough patients to meet expenses can be challenging – it may take time for the practice to fill to a sustainable level.

High Patient Expectations: Members are paying specifically for enhanced access and service. This means you must be available and responsive. Patients might call or message at night or weekends – even if such contact is infrequent, they expect you to be there when needed. You have to be careful to set boundaries to avoid burnout; for example, some concierge docs rotate phone availability with a colleague or hire nursing staff to assist, but if you're solo, it can be essentially a 24/7 commitment to your panel. Failing to meet a patient's expectations could mean they leave the practice (and potentially a hit to your reputation), so there is pressure to go above and beyond consistently.

Limited Scope of Practice: In a primary care concierge or DPC practice, you'll still need to refer patients out for specialty care, hospitalizations, or procedures not done in-office. Patients must carry some form of insurance or be willing to pay out-of-pocket for those needs, which can complicate coordination. While this isn't a direct downside for your practice, it means you often act as a navigator for your patients through the traditional system for anything beyond what you handle. Some concierge physicians coordinate closely with specialists for their patients, which is extra work (albeit part of the promise of comprehensive care). Also, if you enjoy a fast-paced environment or high procedure volume, a small concierge practice might feel too slow or narrow after a while.

Autonomy here is very high – arguably the closest to absolute professional freedom a physician can get in modern practice. You answer mainly to your patients (and of course ethical and standard-of-care norms) rather than corporations or insurance. The schedule is highly in your control: you can decide how many patients to see per day and can often arrange longer visits and more breaks as needed. Many concierge/DPC physicians report a more relaxed daily pace, but with the trade-off of being continuously available by phone/text for urgent issues. The patient mix in a DPC or concierge practice is usually primary care-oriented and often skewed to those who value and can afford this care – possibly more adults with chronic conditions who appreciate close monitoring, or busy professionals who pay for convenience. It may lack the socioeconomic diversity of a general practice, which is something to consider if that's important to you. For career development, you won't have academic titles or a big organization to climb, but you develop strong business acumen and customer service skills. Some concierge doctors become local experts in preventive care or lifestyle medicine because they have time to delve into those areas. You could also expand into a hybrid model (see below) or even eventually grow and hire another physician if your panel demand exceeds your capacity. Just remember, growth must be handled carefully to not dilute the very intimacy that defines the model.

3.8 Telemedicine Roles

Telemedicine roles involve providing patient care remotely, using technology like video calls, phone, or messaging. As a telemedicine physician, you might work for a telehealth company (e.g., doing virtual urgent care or tele-psychiatry), for a hospital system's telemedicine department (such as teleradiology or tele-ICU monitoring), or as part of a medical group that offers virtual visits to its patients. Some telemedicine jobs are full-time and fully remote – you log in from home and see patients via a platform – while others are part-time or integrated with an in-person practice (for instance, a clinic physician might do telehealth one day a week). Telemedicine greatly expanded in the wake of the COVID-19 pandemic and is now considered a permanent and growing part of healthcare delivery. In many specialties (especially primary care, psychiatry, dermatology, radiology), it's possible to practice almost entirely online.

Pros

Geographic Flexibility and Remote Work: Telemedicine is unmatched for location flexibility. You can work from your home, and theoretically from anywhere (as long as you're licensed in the state where patients are). For physicians with personal commitments – say you live in a rural area with limited local opportunities, or you want to be home with young children – telehealth can be a game-changer. Many doctors find the ability to eliminate commutes and practice from a home office incredibly convenient. This flexibility also allows for a better work-life integration; for example, between virtual visits you might be able to briefly check on your family or handle personal tasks, which is harder to do in a clinic setting.

Flexible Scheduling Options: Telemedicine roles can often be tailored to your preferred schedule. There are opportunities for night shifts, weekday hours, part-time weekends – you name it. You might choose to do telemedicine as a supplement to another job (moonlighting) or as your primary gig. Some physicians do telemedicine during off-hours to earn extra or keep a flexible lifestyle. As Dr. Kurt Gilbert noted after switching to full-time telemedicine, "when my shift is over, I'm done", and he could use his lunch break to see his 17-month-old child. That kind of defined stop time and ability to set boundaries can reduce burnout.

Efficiency and Focused Encounters: Virtual visits can be surprisingly efficient. Without the need to physically room patients or wait on them changing gowns, many simple visits (like medication refills, routine follow-ups, minor acute issues) are handled quickly. This can let you see a reasonable volume in less time. Also, telemedicine often handles specific problems – you might address one acute issue per visit – which can be less complex than juggling multiple complaints in an in-person primary care visit. In fields like radiology or pathology, working remotely doesn't change the work much at all, and you can often work undisturbed in your own space.

Expanding Access to Care: From a mission standpoint, telemedicine can be powerful. You might provide care to patients in underserved areas who otherwise travel hours to see a specialist. There's a sense of being on the frontier of a new mode of care, which some find exciting. It's worth noting that most physicians now believe telehealth is here to stay and will be part of almost everyone's practice in some form. By diving in, you gain expertise in a growing arena of medicine, potentially positioning yourself for future leadership in telehealth as it continues to evolve.

Cons

Limited Scope of Practice: Not everything can be managed virtually. Telemedicine works well for straightforward issues – follow-ups for chronic conditions, mental health consultations, minor illnesses like colds or rashes (with pictures). But if a patient has something that requires a hands-on exam (abdominal pain, a suspicious lump to palpate, etc.), you are limited. Often you'll need to refer patients to in-person care if their issue goes beyond what can be evaluated through a screen. This can be frustrating as a clinician, and sometimes for patients who hoped you could solve everything remotely. You have to be comfortable with a practice that may involve a lot of triage and advice, rather than definitive treatments in one encounter.

Reduced Personal Connection: While video visits work, they are not quite the same as sitting with a patient in person. Subtle non-verbal cues or the ability to offer a comforting hand on a shoulder are lost. Some physicians (and patients) find the virtual interaction less fulfilling in terms of rapport. Over time, doing medicine through a screen can feel isolating – you might miss the human contact of an office, both with patients and with colleagues. If you work from home solo, you don't have those hallway consults or chats with staff that can brighten a day.

Technical and Logistical Challenges: Telemedicine is completely dependent on technology – both on your end and the patient's. Technical issues like a bad internet connection, software glitches, or a patient who isn't tech-savvy can derail visits. You'll need to be patient and ready to troubleshoot ("Can you try moving closer to your Wi-Fi router?"). Additionally, you must deal with licensing in multiple states if you want to see patients from across state lines, which can mean maintaining several state licenses (with their fees and CMEs). There are also varying regulations: some states or insurers have different rules about what services can be provided via telehealth. This landscape is improving but still can be a headache to navigate.

Monotony and Ergonomics: Sitting at a computer for long stretches is its own challenge. Telemedicine can become a grind of back-to-back video calls if scheduled poorly. Without the movement inherent in clinic work (going room to room, doing procedures, etc.), some find telehealth days surprisingly exhausting in a sedentary way. Taking care of your ergonomics and building in breaks is crucial. And for those who enjoy using their hands in medicine – procedures, physical exams – telemedicine alone would not be satisfying, as you won't be doing those (except perhaps guiding someone remotely).

Autonomy in telemedicine varies: if you're self-employed or contracting per diem, you might choose your work times freely; clinically, you must follow the telemedicine provider's guidelines and you might be constrained to certain formularies or protocols, particularly in corporate telehealth settings. The schedule can be extremely flexible by design – you might choose shifts that suit you – but when you are on a shift, you might need to handle a high volume of consults rapidly (some services expect 15+ video visits a day). The patient mix for general telemedicine skew towards acute minor issues or routine follow-ups. You might see a lot of similar complaints (e.g., respiratory infections, UTIs, anxiety check-ins) because those lend themselves to telehealth. If you're in tele-specialty, you'll see the cases appropriate for remote management in that field. Over time, you'll become adept at managing what can be done via telehealth and spotting what cannot. In terms of career development, telemedicine is a relatively new field – there aren't traditional "chief of telemedicine" roles in abundance yet, but they are emerging. You could move into telehealth administration or help craft virtual care protocols as you gain experience. Some academic centers now have directors of telehealth programs, so one could parlay experience into such positions. Additionally, being involved in telemedicine now is a bit of being part of the future of medicine, which can be intellectually rewarding. Many physicians keep a hybrid of telemedicine and in-person work to balance the pros and cons – which leads us to hybrid models.

3.9 Hybrid Practice Models

"Hybrid" can refer to any combination of the above practice models or incorporation of multiple professional roles. In essence, a hybrid model is a blend of two or more arrangements. A common example is an academic-private hybrid, where a physician works part-time in a community private practice and also has a university affiliation for teaching or research. Another example is a hybrid concierge practice – some physicians maintain a traditional insurance-based practice while offering a concierge option to a subset of patients (this can be a way to transition slowly). You might also consider your own career a hybrid if, say, you work four days employed by a hospital and moonlight on weekends as a locum tenens or telemedicine doctor. Essentially, hybrid models are about customizing your career to include multiple elements. These arrangements often require careful coordination but can provide the benefits of each model if done right.

Pros

Customized Career Fit: A hybrid path lets you mix and match to suit your interests. Love teaching but also want the earnings and patient continuity of private practice? You can do both by affiliating with a medical school while running a practice – the academic-private hybrid "offers the best of both worlds" when executed well. Similarly, if you enjoy concierge style but don't want to give up serving a broader patient base, a hybrid practice can allow a portion of your panel to be concierge and the rest traditional. This flexibility means you don't have to give up one passion for another.

Diversity and Reduced Monotony: By having multiple roles, your workweek might be more varied. For example, two days a week you might be in clinic, one day in the endoscopy suite, one day teaching residents, and one day doing telemedicine from home. The variety can keep you engaged and prevent burnout. Each role informs the other – your academic work keeps you evidence-based in private clinic; your real-world practice gives you material to teach students.

Broader Professional Network and Skills: Working in different environments (hospital and office, or academic and private, etc.) exposes you to more colleagues and systems. This can broaden your professional network significantly. You also develop a wider skill set – perhaps learning business management from your private practice side and research skills from your academic side. Hybrid physicians often become versatile and can pivot in their career more easily. If one sector experiences a downturn or you need a change, you have a foot in another door already.

Potential for Additional Income Streams or Resources: While we're not focusing on compensation specifics, one practical upside of hybrids is that you might have multiple income sources (e.g., a base salary from a university plus practice revenue or locum pay). Additionally, one role might offer benefits or resources that support the other – for instance, your academic affiliation could grant you access to research labs or medical libraries that enrich your private practice with cutting-edge knowledge.

Cons

Complex Scheduling and Workload: Juggling dual (or multiple) roles is challenging. It requires meticulous planning and time management. You have to ensure the commitments of one job don't conflict with the other. This can mean carefully coordinating clinic days vs. teaching days months in advance. It can be mentally taxing to switch "hats" frequently. Without strong organizational skills, you risk dropping balls – like forgetting a lecture you're supposed to give because you were too absorbed in your practice duties. Essentially, you carry the workload and responsibility of more than one position, which can lead to longer total work hours if not controlled.

Boundary Issues and Conflicts of Interest: Sometimes the two worlds can collide. For example, if you're employed by a hospital part-time and also have a private practice, the hospital might expect your loyalty and for you to refer patients internally, whereas in your practice you might prefer other arrangements. Or if you're academic part-time, you might still have to attend meetings or fulfill certain admin duties even on weeks you're busy with your other job. Role conflict can occur if expectations are not clearly defined with both employers. It's critical to have agreements in place that outline your duties and limits in each role.

Partial Immersion Drawback: In any one environment, you're not there full-time, which sometimes means you're seen as an "outsider" or not fully part of the team. For instance, a hybrid academic may not be on campus every day, so students might find it harder to reach them, or they might miss out on some day-to-day happenings in the department. In private practice, your patients might need to see a colleague on days you're at the university, which can affect continuity. You have to work extra hard to maintain presence in both spheres so that neither group of stakeholders (patients, colleagues, students) feels you're absent too often.

Logistical Overhead: Managing two sets of everything – two offices, two email systems, two sets of performance evaluations – can be a lot of red tape. You might attend double the meetings (faculty meeting and practice partners meeting). Documentation requirements could also double (charts in two systems, etc.). Some hybrids alleviate this (e.g., an academic-private hybrid might use one hospital's system for both roles if the practice is affiliated), but often it's distinct. You'll need to stay organized to keep licenses, CME, credentialing current in both arenas. Burnout is a risk if the combined bureaucracy of both roles becomes overwhelming.

In a hybrid model, autonomy depends on the components – you might have high autonomy in the private portion and low in the employed portion. You will need to be comfortable switching between modes (answering only to yourself vs. to a boss, etc.). The schedule is both a pro and con: it's flexible by design (you created it to include what you want), but day-to-day it might be tightly orchestrated to fulfill all obligations. It's crucial to guard against overcommitment – one seasoned hybrid practitioner advises, "Plan three to four weeks ahead" and don't commit to things you can't follow through. The patient mix and experiences will span settings – perhaps community patients in your practice and complex referrals in your academic role, giving a rich mix. This can enhance your clinical acumen. For career development, hybrids can accelerate your growth in multiple dimensions, but you might advance a bit slower in any one given track since you're part-time there. For example, it may take longer to make full professor if you're only academic half-time, or you might not grow your practice as quickly because you're not there every day. On the flip side, you have more career resiliency – if one avenue slows, the other can take precedence. Hybrids exemplify how modern careers can be non-linear, and they require flexibility, communication, and a clear vision of what you want from each component.

Summary Choosing a practice model is a personal decision, and there is no one-size-fits-all answer. You might prioritize autonomy and decide the freedom of solo or concierge practice is worth the extra responsibility. Or you might value a predictable schedule and team support, making hospital or large system employment attractive. Academic medicine could be your calling if teaching and research inspire you, whereas locum tenens might suit you if adventure and flexibility are what you crave right now. Many physicians will transition between models over their careers – for example, starting employed, then later opening a private practice or moving into academia, or mixing roles to achieve balance.

As a seasoned colleague might say: "Know yourself and what energizes you." If you thrive on independence, consider the models that maximize autonomy. If you dread bureaucracy, a smaller practice might make you happier than a huge system. If work-life balance is paramount, look at settings known for stable hours. It's wise to talk to physicians working in each type of model, ask about their lifestyles and stressors, and even consider trying a short locum stint or telemedicine gig to sample different environments.

Remember that none of these choices is irrevocable. Early in your career, you can course-correct if a setting doesn't fit well. The key is to enter your first job with eyes open to the typical structure, pros, cons, and considerations we've discussed. With that knowledge, you can negotiate wisely, set realistic expectations, and lay the groundwork for a fulfilling career. No matter the model, maintaining your own well-being and sense of purpose is crucial – a happy doctor tends to make for happier patients and a sustainable practice. Good luck as you start this exciting chapter of choosing your path in the world of medicine!

Chapter 4

Preparing for Interviews

Congratulations – you've been offered an interview! Interviews are your opportunity to evaluate potential employers while they evaluate you. This section will help you prepare thoroughly for both in-person and virtual interviews. We'll cover how to present yourself (attire and body language), common interview formats and what to expect, logistics (travel and technology prep), etiquette during the interview, and post-interview follow-up. Good preparation can significantly boost your confidence and performance on interview day.

4.1 Before the Interview: Research and Preparation

Understand the Format: An in-person physician interview can range from a single afternoon to a multi-day on-site visit. Typically, you might start with a dinner or informal meeting the evening before (for longer interviews), followed by a day of interviews with various stakeholders – department heads, potential colleagues, hospital administrators, etc. Some interviews also include a tour of the facility and the community. Academic positions might require you to give a presentation or Grand Rounds. Before the interview, make sure you have an itinerary or agenda. If one isn't provided, don't hesitate to ask the coordinator or recruiter: "Could you please let me know what the interview day will entail and whom I'll be meeting?" Knowing the schedule helps you prepare mentally and perhaps research the people you'll meet.

What to Wear: For any in-person interview, dress professionally – when in doubt, go with business formal attire. This typically means a suit for both men and women. Men should wear a suit (jacket and tie); a neutral color like navy, gray, or black is safe with a light-colored dress shirt. Women can wear a suit (pants or skirt) or a conservative professional dress with a blazer. Aim for professional and comfortable. It's perfectly fine for women to wear pantsuits; whatever makes you feel confident and is appropriate to the setting. Avoid loud colors or flashy patterns; subtle and neat is the goal. Make sure you try on your outfit beforehand and it fits well – you don't want wardrobe malfunctions or discomfort (new shoes broken in, etc.). If you'll be touring clinical areas, some candidates wonder if they should wear a white coat; generally, you do not need to wear a white coat during an interview unless specifically asked to for a clinical observation. The suit is standard. Also, groom well: neat hair, clean nails, and minimal jewelry or fragrance (strong colognes/perfumes can be distracting or problematic for some). These seem like small details, but they contribute to a polished impression.

Travel Logistics: If you are flying or driving in the day before, plan your travel to arrive with plenty of buffer time. Avoid the last flight of the night that could be canceled or delayed – it's recommended to travel a day early if possible. If the hospital is arranging travel, they might handle some of this for you, but double-check times. Choose a hotel close to the interview location to minimize commute stress (often, the employer will put you up at a nearby hotel). Know how you will get from the hotel to the interview site – rental car, taxi, rideshare – and consider doing a test drive or at least a dry run mentally. Plan to arrive at least 20-30 minutes early on interview day. This gives you time to park, find the meeting spot, and compose yourself. It's much better to have a few minutes to breathe (or review your notes) than to rush in panicked because of traffic.

If your interview spans a mealtime or overnight, you might have less formal settings like dinner with physicians or lunch with staff. Even though those can be more relaxed, remember you're still being evaluated. For dinners, business casual attire is often acceptable (if you had formal interviews all day, you can assume your suit is fine for dinner, or you could remove the jacket, but generally maintain a professional look). At any meals, mind your etiquette: be polite to serving staff, don't order alcohol unless your host explicitly encourages it and you are comfortable (one drink maximum in any case), and focus on conversation more than the food. Often the dinner is a chance for them to gauge your personality and fit.

What to Bring: Carry a professional-looking folder or portfolio with a notepad, pen, and a few extra copies of your CV. You probably won't need the CV since all interviewers should have it, but it's good to have just in case. In that pad, have a list of questions you want to ask (so you don't forget). If you have a business card (not common for new grads, but fellows sometimes have them), you can bring some. You do not need to bring copies of transcripts or certificates to a job interview unless they asked (usually those come during credentialing later). Do bring your photo ID (needed if they take you to secure areas or if you end up needing to show ID at HR). If you're giving a presentation, have it on a USB drive or your laptop as needed.

Research the Organization: Before interviewing, thoroughly research the organization. Review the hospital or practice website, read about their mission and values, look up recent news or developments, and try to understand the patient population they serve. If it's a teaching hospital, look at their residency programs and academic affiliations. For private practices, learn about their size, structure, and any unique services they offer. Knowledge of the organization shows genuine interest and helps you ask informed questions.

Know Your Interviewers: If possible, find out who will be interviewing you and research their backgrounds. This is especially important for physician leaders or potential department chairs. Look up their training, publications, and clinical interests on the organization's website or professional platforms like Doximity or PubMed. Understanding your interviewers' backgrounds helps you connect more effectively and shows your thoroughness.

4.2 During the Interview

Professionalism and Enthusiasm: On the day, treat **everyone** you meet with courtesy – from the front desk receptionist to the clinic nurse who shows you around. A common adage is "assume everyone you encounter is part of the interview". Often, hiring committees will informally ask support staff how the candidate behaved. You want to be remembered as gracious and humble. Introduce yourself to each person, shake hands (firm but friendly handshake), make eye contact, and smile. These basic interpersonal skills set a positive tone. Interviews for physicians are often semi-formal conversations. Interviewers may try to put you at ease, but you should still stay professional in your language and demeanor. Avoid slouching or appearing disinterested; show engagement by nodding and maintaining good eye contact. It's natural to be a bit nervous, but try to speak clearly and not too fast. Take a moment to think if you need to – it's perfectly okay to pause briefly before answering a question, rather than rambling off track.

Answering Questions: Common questions in physician interviews include inquiries about your training, your interest in their job, how you handle certain clinical or interpersonal situations, and what you're looking for in a practice. (We will delve into specific questions and model answers in the next section.) When answering, aim to be honest, concise, and structured. Use examples from your experience to illustrate your points. For instance, if asked how you work under pressure, you might briefly recount a busy night on call where you handled multiple sick patients (following a STAR method: situation, task, action, result). Always frame answers in a positive or learning-oriented light – even if talking about a challenge or mistake, emphasize what you learned or how you improved from it. Since many physician interview questions are behavioral (e.g., "Tell me about a time when..."), having a few go-to stories prepared can be very helpful

Prepare Your Own Questions: Almost every interviewer will give you a chance to ask questions. Having thoughtful questions is crucial – it shows interest and insight. Prepare a list in advance, but also tailor it based on who you're speaking with. For example, with a senior physician you might ask about the department's culture or challenges. With an administrator, you could ask about strategic goals for the practice. Here are some strong questions you might consider: - "How would you describe the group's culture and the teamwork among physicians and staff?" - "What are the biggest challenges facing the department (or practice) in the next few years?" - "What does a typical week look like for a new physician here in terms of schedule, call, etc.?" (if not already clarified) - "How are decisions made in the group – for example, about new initiatives or changes in practice?" - If interviewing in a hospital: "How would you characterize the relationship between physicians and administration?" - You can ask individuals about their personal experience: "Dr. X, what do you enjoy most about working here?" – this can provide insight and also help build rapport.

Avoid questions that are too focused on your needs (salary, vacation, etc.) at this stage – those are important, but usually handled once they are seriously considering you or at the offer stage. Also avoid any questions that could come off as presumptive (like asking about minor perks too early). You want to show that you are evaluating them on meaningful factors. **Do not shy from asking about things that matter to you**, though. If call schedule or partnership track is a deal-breaker, it's reasonable to ask about those during the interview day, especially if meeting with HR or practice leadership. You can phrase it diplomatically: e.g., "Can you tell me about the call responsibilities for this position?" or "I read in the job description about a potential partnership – could you elaborate on how that works over time?" It's better to have clarity now than to be surprised later. Just balance these questions with others that aren't solely about your personal benefit – demonstrate you care about the role and team too.

Stay Positive and Professional: No matter how comfortable you might feel with an interviewer, avoid speaking negatively about past employers, training programs, or colleagues. If asked about a difficult situation (like conflict or a case that went wrong), explain candidly but never bad-mouth individuals or institutions – it reflects poorly on you. Instead, focus on the facts or what you learned, not the people. Also, be mindful of confidentiality/HIPAA when giving clinical examples – anonymize details.

Energy and Attitude: Show enthusiasm for the opportunity. Even if by midday you sense this job might not be for you, stay engaged – you are building your professional network with everyone you meet. Also, first impressions can be wrong; you might find your opinion shifts as you learn more. Demonstrating curiosity, passion for your field, and collegiality will leave a good impression. Many employers hire for "fit" as much as for skills, so they want to see that you are someone who will be a positive member of the team.

Handling Nerves: It's normal to be nervous. Preparation will help, as will practicing some mindfulness or positive visualization. Before you walk in, take a deep breath, remind yourself that you are a qualified doctor (they wouldn't be interviewing you if you weren't), and that this is as much about you evaluating them as vice versa. Some find it helpful to do a power pose or other techniques to boost confidence (in private) (Successfully Navigating the Physician Job Interview - PMC). During the day, if you find yourself anxious, focus on listening – really tune in to what each interviewer is saying or asking, which can center you in the moment.

4.3 Virtual Interview Considerations

Virtual interviews (via Zoom, Microsoft Teams, Skype, or other platforms) have become more common, especially in the aftermath of the COVID-19 pandemic. Some employers conduct an initial video interview as a screening step before inviting you on-site, while others might offer completely virtual interview processes. Preparing for a virtual interview is equally important, with some special considerations.

Tech Setup: Well before the interview day, ensure you have the necessary technology ready: - A reliable internet connection is a must. If possible, use a wired Ethernet connection or ensure you have strong Wi-Fi. - A computer with a functioning webcam and microphone. Test them using the same platform (if the interview is on Zoom, do a Zoom test call). Make sure you know how to join the meeting and that any required software is updated. If you haven't used the platform before, install it and practice.

Camera positioning and lighting: Set up your camera at eye level; you don't want it too low (looking up your nose) or too high. Use a stable surface (avoid a wobbly laptop on your lap). Good lighting can make a big difference – ideally face a light source (natural light from a window or a lamp behind the camera) so your face is clear. Avoid having bright lights or windows behind you, which will cast you in shadow.

Choose a quiet, interruption-free environment. The background should be neat and not distracting. A plain wall or a tidy office setting is ideal.

Virtual backgrounds can be used if you can't curate a good real background, but choose a subtle, professional one (or a simple blur). Make sure if you use a virtual background that your face doesn't glitch in and out – that can be more distracting. Often a neutral real background is best. - Use a headset or earphones if your environment has any noise or if your computer microphone isn't clear. This can improve sound quality and help you hear better.

Professional Appearance: Treat a virtual interview like an in-person one in terms of attire. Dress in professional attire head-to-toe, not just from the waist up. This helps you psychologically get into "interview mode" and avoids embarrassment if you need to stand up unexpectedly. Solid colors often work better on camera than busy patterns. Also, have a glass of water nearby in case you need it, but avoid eating or chewing gum.

Eye Contact on Video: This can be tricky – if you stare at the image of the interviewer on your screen, you may not appear to be looking at them due to camera alignment. Try to look into the webcam when you are speaking, as that simulates eye contact from their perspective. You can glance at their face on screen when listening, of course, but frequently return your gaze to the camera. This takes practice; you could do a test recording of yourself to see how it looks.

Eliminate Interruptions: Ensure family members or roommates know you cannot be disturbed. Silence your phone. Close any noisy apps or computer notifications that might pop up (an email ping or calendar alert can disrupt your flow). If you have pets that might bark or jump in your lap, see if you can have them in another space during the call. Technology issues sometimes happen despite best plans – if something occurs (video freeze, etc.), stay calm. Often the interviewers are understanding and will reconnect. It's good to have a backup phone number to reach each other if video fails; you can ask ahead of time for a dial-in number or provide your phone as backup.

Virtual Body Language and Etiquette: Even though you're not in person, body language still comes across. Sit up straight, keep your shoulders relaxed, and try not to fidget. Use head nods and smiles to convey warmth and attention. Avoid the temptation to multi-task on the computer; looking off to the side or typing will be obvious. Additionally, because virtual connections can introduce a slight audio lag, be mindful not to talk over the interviewer. Let them finish their question, maybe give a one-second pause, then respond – this avoids both people speaking at once due to lag. If you notice a delay, you can acknowledge it: "Sorry, I think there was a slight delay. To answer your question..." – a little awareness goes a long way.

The content of your answers and questions in a virtual interview should be the same quality as in-person. Be prepared with the same stories and examples. One advantage of virtual – you can keep a few notes or your CV just out of sight of the camera for quick reference. It's okay to have a bullet list of key points off-screen, but don't rely on reading – it should not look like you're reading a script. Just use it as a prompt if needed. Practice a virtual interview with a friend if you're new to it, to get feedback on your setup and presence.

Finally, treat the virtual interview with the same level of formality: log in a few minutes early, greet everyone politely (*"Hello Dr. Smith, it's nice to meet you"*), and at the end, thank them for their time. The goal is to be memorable for your content and personality, not for any technical hiccups. With preparation, a virtual interview can be just as successful as an in-person meeting.

While virtual interviews have limitations (harder to sense organizational culture, limited facility tours), they can be effective screening tools. If your entire interview process is virtual, consider asking for additional ways to learn about the workplace, such as virtual tours, conversations with potential colleagues, or detailed descriptions of facilities and workflows.

4.4 After the Interview: Follow-Up and Next Steps

Once your interview day (or virtual interviews) are completed, your work isn't done. Post-interview etiquette and follow-up are important for leaving a good final impression.

Thank-You Notes: It's customary to send a thank-you message to those who interviewed you. In the past, handwritten notes were common, but email has become perfectly acceptable and faster. Ideally, within 24-48 hours after the interview, send a brief, personalized thank-you email to the key individuals you spoke with. This typically includes the hiring manager (department chief or practice leader), anyone who would be your direct supervisor, and perhaps a recruiter or HR person who facilitated. If you met multiple people in a panel, you could send a note to the group or individual notes if you have their contacts. Keep it short: express appreciation for their time, reaffirm your interest in the position (if true), and maybe reference something specific from your conversation to make it personal. For example: *"Dear Dr. Smith, Thank you for the opportunity to visit XYZ Health and discuss the cardiology position. I enjoyed learning about your team's approach to patient care, especially the integration of the new heart failure clinic – it aligns with my interests from fellowship. I left impressed with the collegial environment and am very interested in the opportunity to join your group. Please extend my thanks to Dr. Jones as well. I look* *forward to hearing from you. Sincerely, [Name]."* Be sure to spell names correctly and double-check before sending. This follow-up is not just polite; it also serves to reiterate your interest and keep you top-of-mind. (If you are no longer interested after the interview, you should still thank them for their time, but you don't need to gush about interest – you can simply say it was a pleasure to learn about their practice.)

Follow Their Timeline: Often, at the end of interviews, you will be informed of the next steps or timeline. If they say, *"We hope to make a decision in the next two weeks,"* respect that timeline before panicking about not hearing back. It's fine in your thank-you note to also say, "If there is any additional information I can provide, please let me know." If the stated timeline passes and you haven't heard, a gentle follow-up email or call to your contact (recruiter or HR) inquiring about the status is okay. Hiring processes can move slowly, especially with committee decisions and contract approvals, so some patience is required. That said, if another offer or deadline is approaching, you can politely let them know you have another opportunity's timing to consider – sometimes that can expedite a decision if they are interested.

Evaluate the Opportunity: Right after the interview, while it's fresh, it's helpful for you to jot down pros and cons and how you felt about the place. Interviews are as much for you to assess fit as for them. Think about the people you met, the vibe, whether you could see yourself working there. If something felt off, note it and maybe seek clarification (perhaps via another conversation or questions if you advance to offer stage). If you loved it, that's great – but still keep notes to compare with other interviews.

Second Looks or Follow-Up Visits: Occasionally, you might be invited for a second interview or a site visit (especially if the first was virtual). Treat that with equal seriousness. It may be more focused on specifics like meeting future colleagues or seeing housing areas for relocation. It's usually a good sign if you're invited back, meaning you are a finalist.

Negotiation and Offer Stage: If the interview goes well, you may progress to the offer stage. Typically, the employer will call to extend a job offer, often contingent on contract details. This is when discussion about salary, benefits, and contract terms happens. We won't dive deeply into contract negotiation here, but do know that you can negotiate and ask questions. If you have multiple offers, weigh them carefully considering factors like compensation, location, growth opportunities, and gut feeling. It's perfectly acceptable (in fact, advisable) to have an attorney review any physician employment contract before you sign – you can let the employer know you'd like a little time for that review.

By following up courteously and reflecting on each interview experience, you will not only maximize your chances of landing an offer, but you'll also ensure you choose the right fit for your first attending job. Now that we've covered preparation and etiquette, let's move on to common interview questions you might face and how to approach them.

4.5 Interview Questions and Strategic Responses

Interview questions for attending physician positions generally fall into a few categories: personal and motivation questions, behavioral questions, clinical or scenario-based questions, and questions about fit for that particular job. Below, we provide a selection of common questions in these categories, along with guidance or model answers that illustrate strong responses. These are meant to help you craft your own answers by reflecting on your experiences and how you want to present them.

Remember, for behavioral and scenario questions, a helpful technique is the **STAR** method – Situation, Task, Action, Result – to structure your answer as a brief story with a positive outcome or lesson.

1. **Tell me about yourself / Walk me through your background.** This open-ended prompt is almost guaranteed to come up as an icebreaker. It's your chance to deliver a brief elevator pitch about your professional background and interests. A good model answer is concise (1-2 minutes) and focused on your career. For example: *"I'm originally from Texas, completed my medical school at UT Southwestern and now I'm finishing my final year of general surgery residency at Stanford. I've developed a strong interest in surgical oncology through my rotations, and I'll be graduating in June. Outside of work, I'm someone who values teamwork – I was actually one of the chief residents this year – and I enjoy mentoring junior residents. I'm now looking to return to the Houston area to practice, which is what drew me to this opportunity at your hospital."* This kind of answer hits key points: where you are in training, your specialty focus, perhaps a key achievement (chief resident), and a personal tie-in to why you're interested in them (location, for instance). Do mention your specialty and training; don't go into every detail of your CV (they have it already). Keep it professional; this isn't the time for a long personal life story or hobbies (one line about outside interests is fine, but not necessary unless they ask).

2. **"Why did you go into medicine?"** or **"What inspired you to choose [Your Specialty]?"** Interviewers often want to understand your motivation. They are looking for genuine passion and commitment. An ideal answer is truthful and reflects altruistic or intellectually driven motivations rather than only personal gain. For

example: "*I was drawn to medicine because I love science and I love working with people – medicine is the perfect intersection of those. In college, volunteering at a clinic showed me how much impact a caring physician can have on someone's life. As for why I chose pediatrics, during rotations I realized I had a knack for connecting with kids and I felt immense reward in helping children get well and supporting their families. Those experiences confirmed that pediatrics was where I belonged.*" Be honest but avoid answers that focus on external factors like money or prestige. (Virtually no one will admit they chose medicine for money, but even joking about it can leave a bad impression. **Employers want to hear that you have a deeper motivation or commitment.**

3. **Why are you interested in our organization/practice?** This tests whether you've done your homework and where your prior research pays off. Interviewers want to see that you are interested in them, not just any job. A good answer might be: "*Several things stood out to me about this opportunity. First, your hospital's reputation for cardiac care is excellent – the fact that you have a top 100 cardiovascular program and are involved in cutting-edge clinical trials is very exciting. Given my interest in heart failure management, the resources here like the advanced heart failure clinic are a big draw. Second, I have family in the area, so I'm looking to settle here long-term, and I've heard from colleagues that the medical community here is very supportive. Lastly, when I spoke to Dr. X during my visit, I really resonated with the collaborative culture she described. I'm looking for a team-oriented group, and I got the sense this place values that.*" This answer shows you've done homework (mentioning specifics) and that you have personal reasons to be invested (family in area, etc.). Customize your answer to whatever genuinely attracts you: could be the patient population, the growth mode of the practice, the alignment with your training, etc.

4. **Where do you see yourself in 5-10 years?** Employers ask this to gauge your long-term plans and commitment. They often want to know if you're likely to stay and grow with them. The key is to show ambition but also some realism and loyalty. For example: "*In five years, I see myself established as a key member of your neurology team, hopefully having developed a sub-focus in stroke care. I'd like to be involved in some clinical trials or research with our stroke center if the opportunity arises, as research is important to me. In ten years, I hope to have taken on some leadership responsibilities – maybe helping lead the stroke program or being involved in resident education if we have a training program. Most importantly, I see myself taking care of a loyal patient base here and really being part of the community.*" This answer indicates you plan to stick around and contribute. If you

have plans like "I might pursue an MBA" or "I want to be program director," you can mention them if relevant, but avoid anything that suggests you're using the job as a short stepping stone. If you truly don't know, it's okay to say you're focused on finding the right first practice to hone your skills and that you anticipate growing with that practice. If you have a unique plan (e.g., plan to join Doctors Without Borders in 5 years), be cautious – if that's a strong intent, you might want to discuss it, but it could raise concerns about longevity. Tailor your answer to show you envision a future that aligns with the job.

5. **"Why should we hire you?" or "What makes you a good fit for this position?"** This is a prompt to summarize your strengths and how they meet the job's needs. It's a chance to sell yourself confidently (not arrogantly). A structure could be: highlight your clinical competence, your work ethic, and your fit with their team. For example: *"I believe I would bring a strong combination of up-to-date clinical skills and a collaborative spirit to your practice. Through my fellowship, I've trained extensively in the latest endoscopic techniques, which would add to your GI department's capabilities. My mentors have described me as very hard-working and reliable – someone who will go the extra mile for a patient – and I'd continue that here. Culturally, I noticed during my visit that your team values communication and teamwork, which are exactly how I like to practice. I'm also fluent in Spanish, which I know is a valuable asset given the community demographics. In short, I'm ready to hit the ground running and contribute to the growth of the practice."* This answer touches on clinical skill, personal attribute (work ethic), team fit, and even a bonus skill (language). Tailor it to your own profile. The idea is to confidently state that you have what they are looking for, and perhaps a little extra.

Behavioral and Interpersonal Questions

Behavioral interview questions often start with, "Tell me about a time when..." or "Give an example of...". They are designed to see how you handle real-life situations, especially those involving communication, ethics, teamwork, or problem-solving. Always include what you learned or how you resolved the situation to a positive end.

6. **"How do you handle stress or pressure? Can you give an example of a stressful situation you faced and how you coped?"** Physicians' jobs are inherently stressful at times, so expect this question. Choose an example from residency or fellowship where things were intense but you managed effectively. A strong answer: *"I find that I perform well under pressure by staying organized and prioritizing tasks. For instance, during my ICU rotation, we had a night when*

three critical patients arrived almost simultaneously – one code blue, one septic shock, and one post-op bleed. It was overwhelming at first. I took a deep breath and quickly triaged with my team: I led the code blue resuscitation, delegated my co-resident to handle initial sepsis management on the other, and called an attending for backup early. By prioritizing the immediacy of needs and communicating clearly with the nurses and team, we managed all three patients. After the crisis, I also debriefed with the team to check on everyone and see what we could do better next time. I've learned that in stress, staying calm, asking for help when needed, and debriefing afterward are key coping strategies for me." This answer demonstrates composure, teamwork, leadership, and reflection. You could also mention personal coping outside of work (exercise, mindfulness) if relevant, but keep the answer mostly professional.

7. **"Describe a time when you had a conflict or disagreement with a colleague (or supervisor). How did you handle it?"** Conflict resolution is critical in healthcare teams. Pick a situation that isn't overly dramatic (avoid airing any severe dirty laundry) but enough to show you dealt with it maturely. For example: *"During my residency, I had a disagreement with a fellow resident about the management of a patient – I felt strongly that we should involve palliative care for a terminal patient, and my colleague thought it was premature and that the family wasn't ready. We initially debated in front of the team, which in hindsight wasn't the best place. I decided to pause the discussion and later that day, I approached my colleague privately. I acknowledged her perspective and asked if we could talk through our differences. By listening to each other without the stress of rounds, we realized we both wanted what was best for the patient. We ended up reaching a plan to gently introduce palliative care while also continuing active treatment for a trial period, which satisfied both approaches. The key was that I didn't let the disagreement fester or become personal – I communicated openly and tried to understand her viewpoint. In the end, we learned to collaborate better and that improved our teamwork."* This shows you didn't avoid the conflict; you addressed it calmly and worked out a compromise, maintaining respect for your colleague.

8. **"Tell me about a time when you had to deliver bad news or deal with a very upset patient (or family)."** Empathy and communication are being tested here. Think of a scenario where you turned a difficult situation into something positive or at least managed it professionally. For example: *"As a senior resident, I often had to break bad news. One case that stands out is a patient whose cancer had progressed despite treatment. Her family was very hopeful and therefore devastated when we had to discuss stopping curative*

therapy. In that family meeting, I made sure to sit down, use simple language, and give them plenty of space to express emotions. The husband became quite angry initially, saying we 'gave up.' I remained calm and acknowledged how hard this was. I said something like, 'I can't imagine how painful this is for you, and I'm sorry that despite everything, we are here.' I let him vent without interruption. Then I gently explained that what we were suggesting was focusing on comfort to ensure his wife had the best quality time left, rather than treatments that could cause more harm than good. I also got our palliative team member to join and reinforce that we would still actively care for her. By the end of the meeting, the family, though very sad, thanked us for our honesty and compassion. I learned that active listening and empathy are crucial in these situations – sometimes patients and families mainly need to feel heard and cared for, even if the news is not what anyone hoped for." This answer demonstrates compassion, communication skills, and maturity in handling emotional situations.

9. **"Give me an example of a time you made a mistake or were wrong about a diagnosis. How did you handle it?"** This question assesses honesty, humility, and learning from errors. A recommended approach is to own the mistake, show how you fixed or addressed it, and what you learned to prevent future issues. For instance: *"During my second year of residency, I misdiagnosed a case initially. A middle-aged patient came in with atypical chest pain. His initial EKG and troponin were normal, and I attributed the pain to acid reflux and anxiety. I sent him home on antacids. The next day, I found out he returned with a large heart attack. I was mortified that I had missed the early signs. I immediately spoke with my attending about it and we did a case review. I also personally apologized to the patient (who fortunately got timely care on the return visit). I realized that I had anchoring bias – I latched onto his stress and normal tests and didn't fully account for his risk factors. Since then, I've been much more thorough with chest pain, erring on the side of observation or further testing when in doubt. That mistake humbled me, but I'm actually grateful it happened early in my training and that the patient ended up okay. It made me a more cautious and thorough physician, and I always remember that case as a lesson in not dismissing concerning symptoms too quickly."* This answer shows accountability (you admitted the mistake, apologized), reflection, and improvement.

10. **"How do you handle working in a team? Can you give an example of a successful team project or when teamwork was essential in your work?"** Healthcare is a team sport, so illustrate your ability to collaborate. Example: *"Teamwork is central to how I operate. In my ICU rotation, we had a multi-disciplinary daily hud-*

dle with nurses, respiratory therapists, pharmacists, and residents. I remember one particularly challenging patient – a young mother with ARDS on a ventilator. Our team functioned incredibly cohesively: I, as the resident, coordinated her care plan but relied heavily on our RT to adjust the ventilator and our pharmacist to manage sedation and paralytics. We had a moment where her oxygen was dropping and everyone snapped into their roles – one nurse drew ABGs, the RT made vent changes, and I communicated with the attending. Over a week, through collective brainstorming (like trying proning and different vent modes) and each member contributing their expertise, we managed to pull her through. I always made sure to value everyone's input – for instance, a bedside nurse suggested a small change in positioning that actually improved perfusion, which we adopted. That experience reinforced for me that everyone on the team is important. I believe in clear communication, mutual respect, and willingness to help each other out. In fact, I carry that ethos to any team: if I finish my tasks, I'll ask if the nurses need help or if colleagues need a hand, and vice versa. It builds trust and ultimately benefits patient care." This answer highlights collaboration, acknowledging others, and leadership by example.

Clinical and Scenario-Based Questions

Interviewers may pose hypothetical clinical scenarios or ethical dilemmas to see your clinical reasoning and judgment. The key is to talk through your thought process in a structured, logical manner and emphasize patient care and safety.

11. **Clinical Scenario: "You are on call as a new attending and you get a call about a post-operative patient who is deteriorating (e.g., low blood pressure, high heart rate). What do you do?"** In such scenarios, outline your approach systematically. For example: *"First, I would gather as much information as possible immediately – vital signs, output, mental status, etc., and ask the nurse to repeat a blood pressure to confirm hypotension. I'd suspect a possible hemorrhage or sepsis depending on the context (let's say this is a day 1 post-op abdominal surgery patient, I'd worry about internal bleeding). I would tell the nurse I'm coming to see the patient right away and to begin initial measures: establish IV access if not already robust, start fluids, get stat labs including hemoglobin and lactate. On arriving (likely within minutes), I'd assess the patient – quick exam for signs of bleeding (abdominal distension, dressings, drains output), check heart and lung exam. If I suspect hemorrhage, I'd call for blood to be typed and crossmatched and alert the OR team of a potential return to surgery. I'd also page my surgical back-up if I'm alone, or senior partner, to apprise them and get help. Basically, I'd stabilize*

the patient (ABC: airway, breathing, circulation – ensure airway is okay, give oxygen, support BP with fluids or pressors if needed) and diagnose at the same time. If it's unclear, I'd get rapid imaging like an ultrasound of the abdomen to check for fluid. But priority is if I think it's an acute abdomen or bleed, I'd prepare for intervention. Throughout, I'd communicate with the ICU team that this patient might need a transfer to higher level care. So in summary: assess quickly, mobilize resources (call for help early), treat empirically (fluids, blood) while finding the cause, and definitively manage the cause (e.g., re-operate for bleeding)." This answer is a bit long verbally, but you want to demonstrate a organized, urgent approach and that you wouldn't try to handle it solo without backup if appropriate.

12. **Ethical Scenario: "You find out that a colleague in your group has been writing prescriptions for family members in a manner that skirts the rules, or perhaps coming to work impaired. What would you do?"** This type of question assesses professionalism and willingness to act in difficult ethical situations. A good approach: *"Patient safety and ethical practice would be my top concern. If I observed behavior suggesting a colleague is practicing unsafely or unethically, I would feel obligated to address it. The exact approach might depend on the situation. If I directly saw a colleague who appeared impaired (say slurring words or smelling of alcohol during a shift), I would immediately ensure that patient care responsibilities are covered – perhaps by discreetly alerting our chief or medical director on call – because patient safety is urgent. Then I would express concern to the colleague, in private if possible, that they don't seem well and shouldn't continue working right now. If it's a pattern or something like writing improper prescriptions, I would probably approach the colleague first if I have a good rapport, and say I've noticed this and am concerned it could harm their career and patient trust. Many times, impairment or boundary-crossing can be a sign someone needs help, so I'd try to be compassionate. However, if it's clearly beyond my ability to handle or they rebuff help, I would escalate to leadership (department chair or our physician wellness/assistance program) as per our professional guidelines. In summary, I'd try to ensure no patients are harmed, encourage the colleague to get help or correct the issue, and involve the appropriate supervisory channels in a timely manner. I know it can be tough to report a colleague, but ultimately our duty is to patients and upholding standards."* This answer shows you prioritize safety and ethics over the discomfort of confronting a peer, and you'd use proper channels, showing integrity.

13. **"How do you approach informed consent and involving patients in decisions?"** This question gets at communication and ethics. A model answer: *"Informed consent is a process, not just a*

form. I make sure to take time with patients when a major decision or procedure is at hand. My approach is to explain the diagnosis or problem in plain language, then discuss the proposed intervention – for example, what the surgery entails or what a treatment would involve – along with the risks, benefits, and alternatives, including what happens if we do nothing. I encourage questions and check for understanding by asking patients to repeat back in their own words what they understand, which can reveal if I need to clarify something. I also try to gauge the patient's values and what matters to them – some patients value quality of life over longevity, etc., which might influence decisions. If a patient has decision-making capacity, I always respect their autonomy. If they decline a recommended treatment, I don't coerce; I make sure they understand the implications, then we find the best plan we can. And I document the consent discussion thoroughly. In summary, I see it as a collaborative conversation to empower the patient to make informed choices, rather than just getting a signature on a consent form." This shows your communication skill and respect for patient autonomy.

14. **"What would you do if a patient or family member openly disagrees with your recommended treatment plan?"** This checks how you handle patient-centered care. A good answer: "*I would first make sure I understand why they disagree. I'd ask open-ended questions to get at their concerns or reasons. For instance, if I recommend a certain medication and the patient refuses, maybe they had a bad side effect in the past or are worried about cost. If a family disagrees with a plan, perhaps they have cultural beliefs or misunderstandings about the prognosis. So I'd listen actively and empathetically. Once I understand their perspective, I'd address it respectfully. If it's a misunderstanding, I'd provide more information or clarify. If it's a value conflict, I'd see if we can adjust the plan in a way that still meets the medical goals but is acceptable to them. For example, some patients might refuse blood transfusions (for religious reasons); I'd then discuss alternatives like erythropoietin or volume expanders and involve ethics if needed. The key is not to be defensive. Ultimately, I aim to partner with patients. If after thorough discussion, the patient still disagrees and it's within their rights (i.e., not a matter of incapacity or public health risk), I will respect their decision. I would document the conversation and make sure they know the door is open to revisit. So in short: listen, understand, educate, and try to reach a mutual agreement. If not possible, respect their autonomy and do the best with the plan they are willing to follow.*" This demonstrates patience, empathy, and commitment to shared decision-making.

15. **"How do you stay current with medical knowledge and advancements in your field?"** Lifelong learning is critical in medicine.

An answer: *"I make it a point to engage in continuous learning. I read journal articles regularly – for example, I subscribe to the Journal of Hospital Medicine and try to review key articles each month. During residency, I developed the habit of following clinical guidelines and updates (like the latest ACC/AHA guidelines in cardiology, etc.). I also attend at least one major conference a year in my specialty – I find that's a great way to learn about cutting-edge developments and network with colleagues. Additionally, I participate in weekly CME activities; in fellowship we had a board review series that I plan to continue with question banks for self-study. I'm also active in an online physician community (like specialty forums) where people discuss challenging cases – that often prompts me to read up on things. So through journals, conferences, CME, and everyday curiosity, I stay up-to-date. I believe in evidence-based practice and know that medicine evolves quickly, so I take responsibility for continually updating my knowledge."* This assures them you won't stagnate and will bring current best practices to the job.

These sample questions cover a broad range. When answering any interview question, be genuine – interviewers can usually tell if someone is being insincere or overly rehearsed. It's okay to take a moment to think and then answer methodically. If you don't have a particular experience asked about (e.g., "Tell me about a research project" and you haven't done one), be honest and pivot to a related experience or an expression of interest to learn. Practice answering these aloud before your interviews; it will help solidify your narratives. With solid preparation, you'll be able to adapt to even unexpected questions.

4.6 Red Flags to Watch for During the Interview and Offer Process

While you evaluate job opportunities, it's important to keep an eye out for warning signs or "red flags" that a position or employer may not be all it seems. These red flags can appear during interviews, in communication with the employer, or when reviewing the contract. Trust your instincts: if something feels off, investigate further. Here are some common red flags and what they might mean:

High Turnover in the Position or Department: If you learn (or observe) that the practice has a revolving door of physicians, take note. For example, if during your interview the practice mentions you're filling a spot that's been vacated multiple times in a short span (e.g., "We've had three doctors leave in the past two years"), that's a red flag. High turnover could indicate underlying problems such as a toxic work culture, overwork, poor management, or an unsustainable compensation model. It's worth politely asking, "Do you know why those physicians left?" Their answer may be revealing – if they seem uncomfortable or give vague explanations, be cautious. You might also ask the remaining physicians about their experience. While every group can have some turnover (retirements, spouse relocation, etc.), a pattern of short tenures is concerning .

Negative Talk or Blame: Pay attention to how your potential future colleagues and bosses talk about the workplace and each other. If an interviewer, for instance, bad-mouths a partner who left, or complains extensively about colleagues or hospital administration, it's a red flag about the culture. You want to join a team that treats each other with respect. An interview should focus on positives of the opportunity; if instead you hear a lot of negativity or office politics, you may be walking into a dysfunctional environment. Similarly, if they speak ill of previous job candidates or other employees, consider how they might speak of you in the future. Look for a culture of support, not blame.

Vague or Evasive Answers: If you ask direct questions about important issues (like call schedule, patient volume expectations, support staff, or how compensation works) and you get non-answers or lots of vagueness, that's a concern. For instance, if you ask, "How many patients am I expected to see in a day?" and the response is, "Oh, don't worry about that, you'll be as busy as you want to be," without specifics, they might be hiding something or not have clear standards. Transparency is key. If terms about call duties, partnership, or bonus structure aren't clearly addressed when you inquire, you should be wary. Employers who dodge questions or change the subject may be glossing over unpopular aspects of the job. Keep pressing politely for clarity; if it's still murky, that's a red flag.

Unclear or Complex Compensation Model: Compensation that is extremely complicated or not clearly explained can be a red flag. For example, if the offer uses lots of jargon (WRVU conversions, guarantee with "clawback" clauses, tiered bonuses) and they can't provide straightforward examples or projections, be cautious. Lack of transparency in pay structure is a common complaint. Also, if it's a private practice partnership track, but they can't tell you what the buy-in entails or what the recent partners' incomes have been, that's concerning. Vague promises like "You'll make partner in a couple years and then your income will skyrocket, trust us" need more detail – ask for numbers. If they won't give them, red flag. Essentially, you should be able to understand how you will earn your income and what the realistic expectations are; if not, you could be signing up for disappointment.

Productivity Extremes or Imbalances: If during your visit you sense that the practice expectations are extreme (e.g., every doctor seeing an extraordinarily high number of patients per day or doing 1:1 call every other night), that may lead to burnout. One hint can be if one or two physicians seem to carry the bulk of the work or are "super-producers" while others struggle – this could mean an unfair distribution of patients or an inequitable practice style. For example, a senior partner might be taking all the lucrative cases. If new patients or referrals aren't distributed evenly, new physicians could be left building a practice with little support. Ask how new patients are assigned and how busy a new doctor typically is in month 6 or 12. If they hedge or if you meet a junior doctor who quietly hints they're not as busy as they hoped, pay attention.

Inadequate Resources or Outdated Facilities: This might come out if you tour the clinic/hospital. If you notice very outdated equipment, or if you ask about something like EMR and they say "Oh, we don't have an EMR, we still use paper charts," (rare these days but possible in some private offices), consider what that means for your practice. Lack of support staff is another red flag – e.g., "you'll have to do without a medical assistant for half the day" or "we're short on nursing support." If they expect you to function without the tools needed for quality care or to take on roles outside your physician duties (like lots of clerical work due to no support), that's concerning. Modern, well-run practices invest in technology and support to help physicians perform at their best. If those are lacking, you might face frustration.

Lack of Transparency or Delayed Offers: The process itself can reveal red flags. If an employer drags their feet excessively or is disorganized (losing paperwork, not returning calls) during recruitment, it could reflect their internal organization. Worse, if they pressure you to sign a contract quickly without giving you time to review, that's a major red flag. You should always have time (at least a couple of weeks) to review a contract and even seek legal counsel. If someone says "We need you to sign this offer within 48 hours or it's off the table," be very wary – a reputable employer knows this is a big decision and will grant a reasonable window. Similarly, if during contract negotiation they promise to send a revised contract and weeks go by with silence until you prod them, it may hint at bureaucratic delays or lack of priority on their end.

Overemphasis on "We're like a family here, trust us" without details: This one can be subtle. It's nice to hear that a team has a family-like atmosphere, but sometimes toxic workplaces use that trope to gloss over structural issues (like expecting overtime without additional pay, or not having clear policies by assuming everyone will just work it out informally). If every question you ask is answered with "We're flexible, we're like family," try to get specifics. For instance, if you ask about work hours and they say "We don't micromanage hours, we're like family," they might actually expect you to stay until everything's done, even if that's very late. A healthy culture can feel like family but will still have clarity and professionalism.

Avoidance of Letting You Talk to Current Physicians: If they do not let you have any private or candid interaction with physicians currently in the practice, that could be intentional to prevent you from hearing negatives. On most site visits, you'll meet other docs – often over lunch or in their office – and that's your chance to ask, "How do you like working here?" If the schedule is arranged such that you're always escorted and never get a minute alone with anyone, or they only let you meet "cheerleaders," it might be staged. You can later try to contact a recent former physician of the group (perhaps through networks) to get an unfiltered opinion. If no one is allowed to speak freely, caution.

Gut Feeling of Disorganization or Bad Culture: Beyond specific red flags, trust your gut. If people seemed unhappy when you visited (maybe staff were complaining or the physicians looked burned out), or if the process was chaotic (they forgot you were coming, etc.), weigh that in. One candidate's red flag might be another's trivial issue, but generally, if you sense a lack of professionalism or enthusiasm on their part, that's a sign. A well-run place will try to impress you too and will be prepared and cordial.

Don't ignore red flags just because you like other aspects (like a good salary or location). Instead, investigate them: ask more questions, talk to others, request another visit if needed. Sometimes there are reasonable explanations, but you deserve to have the full picture before signing on.

Finally, if you identify red flags but still are considering the job, bring them up during negotiations. For example, if the non-compete is too broad, negotiate it down. If call expectations seem extreme, ask if there's a plan to hire more or compensate for heavy call. An employer's response to these concerns will also tell you a lot. A great employer will acknowledge issues honestly and perhaps offer solutions (e.g., "Yes, we've had turnover, but that was due to two retirements; we can connect you with our longest-tenured doc to discuss"). A problematic employer might dismiss your concerns or act offended that you asked – which itself is a red flag.

In sum, being vigilant about red flags is an important part of your due diligence. You are interviewing them as much as they are interviewing you. If most signs are positive, wonderful. But if you see multiple red flags and no good resolutions, it may be wise to walk away. It's better to restart a job search than to enter a job that could make you unhappy or compromise your career early on. There are plenty of fish in the sea, and with your skills in demand, you can afford to be selective and ensure the job you choose is one where you can thrive.

Chapter 5

Compensation

Starting your first attending job is exciting – and a little daunting. Beyond practicing medicine, you suddenly face salaries, bonuses, contracts, and benefits that may feel like a foreign language. This chapter breaks down those complex topics.

5.1 Overview of Compensation Models

When evaluating a job offer, one of the first things to understand is how you will be paid. Physician compensation isn't one-size-fits-all – there are several common models, each with its own logic. The main types include salary-based, RVU-based, productivity-based (e.g. percent of billings), hybrid models, and even global budget arrangements. Knowing the basics of each will help you make sense of your offer and set realistic expectations.

Straight Salary (Guaranteed Base)

A straight salary model pays you a fixed annual amount, usually in regular paychecks. It's simple – you know exactly what you'll earn, which can feel reassuring for a new physician. Salary models are common in large health systems, academic centers, the Veterans Affairs (VA) system, and HMOs. Sometimes there's a minimum guaranteed salary for a year or two, often called a "income guarantee," especially for new grads.

Pros: It's stable and "worry-free" – you don't have to stress about meeting volume targets each month. You can focus on patient care without thinking about how each visit affects your paycheck. Salary guarantees are currently the most prevalent model for new physicians starting out.

Cons: Pure salary offers no direct reward for productivity. An eager, hardworking doctor makes the same as one doing the bare minimum, which may discourage extra effort or efficiency. In a group setting, very high producers might feel they're subsidizing others.

Salary + Bonus: Many employers add an incentive on top of base salary. For example, you get a fixed base of \$200,000, plus eligibility for a bonus if you meet certain goals (which could be productivity, quality measures, patient satisfaction, etc.). This hybrid gives stability with some upside. Always ask how the bonus is calculated, the conditions to earn it, and whether it's guaranteed or discretionary. A base salary plus bonus is currently one of the most popular methods of pay – it provides security while still motivating you to hit targets (assuming the targets are reasonable).

Productivity-Based

"Eat what you kill," as the saying goes. A productivity-based model means your pay directly reflects the amount of work or revenue you generate. There are a few ways this is done:

By Collections: You get paid a certain percentage of what you bill (or what the practice collects from your work). For example, a practice might pay you 30% of your collections. If in a month you generate \$100,000 in collected charges, you earn \$30,000. This is straightforward in theory but can be problematic – if payers delay or deny payments, your income suffers. If using billings, you have to consider the practice's typical collection rate (e.g., if they only collect 60% of charges, a percent-of-billing model effectively pays you on 60% of your work).

By RVUs: Many institutions use Relative Value Units (particularly work RVUs) to measure physician work. Under an RVU model, each service you provide is assigned a value (RVU), and your compensation is a set dollar amount per RVU. For instance, if you have a contract paying \$50 per RVU and you accumulate 5,000 RVUs in a year, you'd earn \$250,000. Often there's a base salary with RVU "bonus": e.g., a base salary up to a threshold of 4,000 RVUs, then additional pay for RVUs beyond that. RVU models are common in hospitals and large groups – they reward output while insulating you from collection issues (the hospital takes on the risk of actually collecting the money). We'll discuss RVUs more in a moment.

Pros: Productivity models reward extra effort – the more patients you see or procedures you do, the more you earn. This can be very lucrative if you're efficient and willing to put in more hours. It also encourages entrepreneurial behavior: physicians have incentive to build the practice, bring in new patients, and perhaps be more mindful of expenses since some models might subtract overhead costs. Many young specialists like the idea of "eating what you kill" because it feels fair and has no ceiling.

Cons: The downside is pressure and competition. In a purely productivity-based group, physicians might become overly competitive, since one person's gain could feel like another's loss. It may deter collegiality – for example, doctors might be reluctant to share patients or cover for each other, knowing it could reduce their own numbers. Also, not all productivity is within your control (clinic flow, support staff, payer mix can all affect your output). If the model is based on collections, you carry risk for things outside your control like insurance denials or hospital billing efficiency. If you're offered a collections-based pay, ask about the group's typical collection percentage and lag time. Know the payer mix too – e.g., mostly Medicare/Medicaid can mean lower reimbursement per work unit. Moreover, burnout can be a risk – pure productivity models may encourage longer hours and more services to boost income, which can lead to fatigue or ethical dilemmas (e.g., pressure to upcode or over-utilize services). Outcomes or quality aren't directly rewarded in this model, only volume.

RVU-Based Models (a type of productivity model)

RVUs (Relative Value Units) deserve special mention. In Medicare's system, every CPT code (service/procedure) is assigned an RVU value. For compensation, often the work RVU (wRVU) component is used as the measure of your productivity. Unlike billing, which depends on payer rates, RVUs are payer-neutral. So, an RVU model pays the same regardless of whether the patient is insured or Medicare or uninsured – this can be good if you serve a poorer population (you're not penalized financially for low reimbursement rates), but bad if you practice in a wealthy area where collections would be very high. Many hospital-employed positions use wRVU models because they align with internal metrics and ensure physicians in different specialties or departments are evaluated on effort, not just revenue.

How RVU pay works: Typically, your contract assigns a dollar per RVU (the conversion factor). Often it's around the Medicare rate. For example, if the conversion factor is ~$33 per RVU (Medicare's ballpark) and you perform a service worth 3 RVUs, the employer values that at about $99. In practice, private employers might use a higher conversion (e.g., $45/RVU) to be competitive. Some jobs set a baseline salary with an RVU target: e.g., a $200k base salary for 5,000 RVUs/year, and then $45 per RVU for any RVUs beyond 5,000. Alternatively, if you produce less than the target, sometimes there's no penalty in year 1, but in future years your salary might adjust down if you consistently underproduce.

Example: Suppose you're a general surgeon. Your contract pays $60 per wRVU. You perform a certain procedure that is 10 wRVUs each. If you do 100 of those in a year ($100 \times 10 = 1,000$ RVUs), that yields $60,000. Meanwhile, each clinic visit or smaller procedure adds RVUs too. Over the year, all your various services' RVUs accumulate. Let's say you end the year with 6,000 wRVUs total. At $60/RVU, that's $360,000. If your base was $300k with a threshold of 5,000 RVU, you would have earned $300k + (1,000 extra RVUs × $60) = $360k.

Ensure you know what counts toward your RVUs (all patient encounters? some jobs exclude certain services). Clarify if there are qualifiers – e.g., sometimes an RVU bonus only pays out if other conditions are met (like not going over a certain expense budget). Also, ask if there's a grace period for ramp up. Many jobs guarantee salary for year 1 then switch to RVU in year 2; check how that transition works and look at how other new hires have fared. A good rule from one expert: "If you can't determine how much you will earn while brushing your teeth, the plan is too complex.". In other words, the compensation formula should be clear enough that you can roughly calculate your own paycheck.

Finally, remember that RVU-based compensation is very common in procedure-oriented specialties (surgery, radiology, etc.) and can be quite lucrative there, but in primary care, pure RVU might undervalue important work like care coordination or longer counseling visits. Many primary care positions now incorporate quality or value incentives to counteract that.

Equal Shares Model

In some private group practices (often single-specialty groups), you might encounter an equal shares model. This means after the group's expenses are paid, the leftover profit is split equally among the physicians. For example, if a group of 5 doctors has net income of $2 million after expenses, each gets $400k. This model treats everyone the same, regardless of individual production.

Pros: It's administratively simple and fosters unity – physicians feel like true partners, not competitors. It discourages overutilization because doing more doesn't personally enrich you unless the whole group does well. It can promote a collegial atmosphere where tasks like teaching, administration, or lower-revenue services (which benefit the practice or patients) are valued since everyone shares the results.

Cons: The obvious downside: hard-working or highly productive doctors may feel dragged down. There's little incentive to go the extra mile if you don't directly benefit. Conversely, a lower-producing physician "rides on the coattails" of others. This can breed resentment if there's a large disparity in effort. Many groups use equal shares only once partners are established, and often only if everyone is contributing similarly. Newcomers might start on a different formula and only become equal partners after proving themselves. Equal-share works best in cohesive groups with similar work ethics and where the services provided by each doctor (even if some generate less revenue) are seen as equally necessary for the practice's mission.

Hybrid Models

In reality, many compensation structures are hybrid – blending elements of salary, productivity, and possibly quality incentives. For instance, a common model is "Base Salary + RVU Bonus + Quality Bonus." You might have a comfortable base pay, and then at year-end get additional compensation if you exceeded a certain RVU threshold and met some quality metrics. Or a practice might pay a lower base salary but give you a percentage of collections after covering your base (like a draw).

Another hybrid is capitation blends, seen in some HMOs or multi-specialty groups: the practice receives a flat monthly amount per patient (capitation) which covers their care, and physicians might then get bonuses for cost efficiency or for keeping referrals in-house. Hybrids attempt to balance security and incentive. As health care moves toward "value-based" care, many employers add bonuses for quality measures, patient satisfaction, or panel management, in addition to volume-based pay.

In certain systems (like government hospitals, the military, or Kaiser Permanente), there is essentially a global budget for physician compensation. In these cases, doctors are often pure salaried (sometimes with small bonuses) because the organization is given a fixed budget to care for a population. For example, the entire Department of a hospital might have a fixed pool for salaries, not tied to individual RVUs. Global budget models emphasize cost containment and teamwork – they are more common in integrated health systems or countries with national health budgets. The upside is stability and potentially more focus on quality; the downside is usually lower potential earnings compared to a high-performing productivity-based environment, and minimal financial reward for seeing extra patients beyond what's expected.

Tip: No compensation model is perfect. Always consider fairness and transparency. If a plan is extremely convoluted or if you cannot get a straight answer on how you'll be paid – that's a red flag. Most new physicians will find their initial offers are pretty standard for the region and specialty (employers usually peg offers to market surveys). In fact, 99% of the time, your starting pay will be in line with what similar docs in similar settings get. Focus less on which model a job uses and more on whether the overall offer meets your needs and whether the practice is a good personal fit. A high salary won't make you happy in a dysfunctional job, and a great workplace can sometimes compensate for slightly lower pay, especially early in your career.

5.2 Billing and Coding Basics: Getting Paid for What You Do

No matter the model, understanding billing and coding basics will empower you. In many systems, your work effort is quantified by what you code. Every patient encounter or procedure is assigned a CPT code and ICD diagnosis. Those CPT codes carry RVUs, which in turn determine how much the insurer pays. In other words, coding drives your revenue and compensation. Ensure your documentation supports the level of service so you're not under-coding (leaving money on the table) or over-coding (which is illegal). Many new doctors assume coding is "the billing department's job," but your coders can only bill based on what you document. So, learning the basics of E/M coding, procedure codes, and modifiers is worthwhile – it helps you get paid for the work you actually do. Don't worry, you don't need to be a pro coder, but do pay attention in any coding orientation your job provides. It can literally pay off.

Let's break down the basics: CPT codes, ICD-10 codes, RVUs (again), modifiers, documentation, and common pitfalls in coding.

CPT and ICD-10: The Languages of Billing

Every patient encounter generates codes: at minimum, a procedure/service code and a diagnosis code.

CPT Codes (Current Procedural Terminology): CPT codes are five-digit numeric codes that represent medical services and procedures you perform – for example, 99213 for an office visit, 93000 for an EKG, appendectomy has its own code, etc. They are maintained by the American Medical Association and used universally in the U.S. for billing. Think of CPT codes as the "what you did" – E/M visits, surgeries, imaging, etc., each have CPT codes. If you do two procedures, you report two CPT codes (possibly with modifiers, see below). CPT is a uniform language for services that allows accurate reporting and billing across different insurers and systems.

CPT codes also determine RVUs (Medicare assigns RVU values to each CPT – so CPT and RVU are linked). For instance, CPT 99214 corresponds to ~1.92 work RVUs.

There are different categories of CPT codes (Category I for most services, Category II for optional tracking codes, Category III for emerging tech), but as a clinician you'll mostly use Category I codes.

Example: A level 3 new patient visit is CPT 99203. A knee X-ray is CPT 73060. Each is a standardized definition so any biller or payer recognizes it.

ICD-10 Codes: While CPTs describe what you did, ICD-10 codes describe why you did it – the diagnoses or conditions. ICD-10 (International Classification of Diseases, 10th Revision) is a system of alphanumeric diagnosis codes. For example, J20.9 = acute bronchitis, E11.65 = type 2 diabetes with hyperglycemia. These codes justify the medical necessity of the CPT codes. Insurers look for ICD codes to match the services – e.g., a CPT for "appendectomy" should be accompanied by an ICD-10 code for "appendicitis" as the indication.

In the U.S. we use ICD-10-CM for diagnosis coding. Codes can range from 3 to 7 characters long (more digits = more specific).

ICD-10 is important for billing because if the diagnosis doesn't support the service (for instance, billing a CPT for a foot x-ray with an ICD code for sore throat would get denied), you won't get paid. It also affects risk adjustment and quality metrics.

Example: You see a patient for uncontrolled hypertension. You'd bill an E/M CPT for the visit (e.g., 99214) and link it to ICD-10 code I10 (essential hypertension). Both codes go on the claim.

Why you should care: As a physician, you'll usually select diagnosis codes in your note or EHR, and sometimes procedure codes. If you choose too vague a diagnosis, claims may be denied for lack of medical necessity. If you pick the wrong CPT (e.g., a higher level visit than your documentation supports), you could be upcoding and risk audits. Understanding CPT/ICD helps you work with coders to ensure your documentation matches the codes billed.

The RBRVS and RVUs (Payment Building Blocks)

We discussed RVUs in the compensation section, but here's how they function in billing: Medicare's Resource-Based Relative Value Scale (RBRVS) assigns every CPT a total RVU value (which is the sum of work RVU, practice expense RVU, and malpractice RVU). Insurers (including Medicare) then multiply that by a conversion factor (dollars per RVU) to determine payment. In simpler terms: * Each CPT has a relative weight (RVU). Harder or more resource-intensive services have higher RVUs. * There are adjustments for geography (since practice costs vary by region). * The conversion factor (CF) – around $32-$34 for Medicare in recent years – converts RVUs to dollars.

For example, CPT 99214 (moderate complexity office visit) might have ~3 total RVUs. If CF = $33, Medicare pays about $99 for it. CPT 99213 (lower complexity) has fewer RVUs and pays maybe ~$70. A complex surgery might have 50 RVUs, paying ~$1,650, etc. As a physician, you don't need to calculate RVUs for each service (your billing software does that), but understanding that time/complexity = RVUs = payment is key. It also underscores why coding level appropriately matters: If you consistently undercode visits (e.g., coding level 3 visits as level 2), you leave RVUs (and money) on the table. Conversely, overcoding can trigger penalties.

Modifiers: The Little Two-Digit Codes That Matter

Modifiers are two-character suffixes (numeric or alphanumeric) added to CPT codes to provide extra info. They can affect whether you get paid appropriately. Common examples:

- **-25 modifier:** Indicates a "significant, separately identifiable E/M service by the same physician on the same day as another procedure." In practice, if you see a patient and do a procedure (e.g., office visit + skin biopsy), you append -25 to the E/M visit's CPT to tell the payer the visit was above and beyond the procedure. Without it, the insurer might bundle the visit into the procedure and not pay for the visit. Using -25 correctly can legitimize getting paid for both a procedure and an office visit on the same day.
- **-59 modifier:** Indicates distinct procedural services. It's used to unbundle services that are normally bundled, when appropriate, by showing they were separate. For example, two procedures same day that are normally considered together – if truly separate, -59 can indicate that.
- **Other modifiers:** -26 (professional component), -TC (technical component), -50 (bilateral procedure), -LT/RT (left/right side), -LTGA (teaching status modifiers for Medicare), etc.

Modifiers can be the difference between full reimbursement, reduced payment, or denial. For instance, forgetting a -25 modifier is a common mistake that leads to the E/M visit not being paid at all. Likewise, misusing modifiers (like adding -59 inappropriately) can be viewed as abusive. When you perform multiple services, minor procedures, or special circumstances, think "Do I need a modifier on any of these codes?" If you're not sure, ask your coder or use coding resources. It's an area where many new physicians make mistakes that cost their practice revenue.

Documentation

Accurate coding goes hand-in-hand with proper documentation. Your documentation in the medical record must justify the codes billed – for both compliance and to defend in case of audit. This is especially true for E/M visit levels and any procedure details. Key points:

- **Linking diagnoses to services:** Ensure your note clearly states the assessments and why procedures were done. Coders will assign ICD-10 codes based on your documented diagnoses. If you list "chest pain" in the note but bill an upper endoscopy, an auditor will scratch their head unless the note explains the connection. Always clearly document why a procedure or test was needed.

- **Supporting E/M levels:** For clinic visits, the level (e.g., 99213 vs 99214) often depends on the complexity, history, exam, and decision-making. If you routinely bill higher levels, make sure your documentation includes the required elements (review of systems, past history, complexity of decision, etc.). "Code what you do, and do what you code." Don't underdocument. If you provided a service, document it so you can code it. For example, if you spent extra time counseling and want to bill a higher code for time, note the total minutes and that >50% was counseling.
- **Procedure documentation:** If you do a procedure, chart the details (size of lesion removed, technique, findings, any complications). These details often determine the CPT code or modifier use.

Solid documentation not only ensures proper reimbursement but also protects you legally and compliance-wise. It provides the necessary information for correct code assignment. Inadequate documentation can lead to claim denials or downcoding (payers reducing the level). For example, if you bill a complex visit but your note is very sparse, an insurer might only pay for a simpler visit. Moreover, good documentation prevents rejections and delays – insurers won't have to request more info if everything needed is in the note

Pitfalls to avoid: * **"Cloning" notes or templating too heavily:** While using templates is efficient, be careful of generic notes that don't reflect the specific visit. Payers are wary of notes that look copy-pasted. * **Forgetting to close charts or sign notes:** An unsigned note can be considered incomplete, which might invalidate the billing. * **Not linking diagnoses:** In some electronic claim systems, you must explicitly link each CPT to the relevant ICD-10. Make sure, for example, your laceration repair CPT is linked to the "laceration" diagnosis code, not to "diabetes" on the problem list.

Remember, thorough documentation = accurate coding = fair reimbursement. It also helps in case of any future audits or questions – you'll have confidence that your records support your billing. As one source notes, comprehensive documentation bridges the information to correct code assignment, ensuring you're paid fairly for your work while guarding against audits or disputes

Common Coding Mistakes

Under-coding E/M visits: Many new docs play it safe and bill a lower level than they actually provided (e.g., coding all visits as 99213). This can significantly reduce revenue over time. If your work was a 99214, don't shy away from coding it – just make sure your documentation supports it. On the flip side, don't default everything to a high level without justification.

Not using modifiers when appropriate: As mentioned, failing to append -25 when you do a procedure with a visit, or -59 for separate procedures, is very common. This leads to missed charges (services you did but didn't get paid for). Train yourself to think "I did two things – do I need a modifier to tell the story?"

Outdated codes or rules: Coding rules change annually. Using obsolete CPT codes (e.g., billing a code that was deleted this year) will cause denials. Keep your code lists and superbills updated. Your clinic's EHR usually updates the code database, but be mindful if you carry forward old code shortcuts.

Diagnosis coding and medical necessity mismatches: Always ensure the ICD-10 diagnoses on the claim support the CPTs. If you order a test or do a procedure, make sure you list the indication in your note and on the order. Medicare in particular is strict about covering services only for approved indications. For example, an EKG for "routine screening" might not be covered, but for "chest pain" it is.

Missing charges: In a busy day, it's easy to forget to bill for something you did (like a simple in-office test or a vaccine). Some studies show practices miss capturing many billable services. Review your day's encounters to ensure everything was coded. Many EMRs help by prompting for common add-on codes (e.g., did you do a rapid strep test but not code it?).

You don't need to be a coding expert overnight, but pay attention and ask questions. Use your coding staff as teachers – a good biller or coder can give you feedback if you consistently make an error. Over time, you'll develop a feel for coding correctly. Accurate coding is not "gaming the system" – it's ensuring you (and your employer) are compensated for the care you provide, and it's important for the financial health of your practice. As one article put it, lost revenue from poor coding affects even employed physicians by limiting resources and potentially reducing bonuses. So it truly pays to pay attention to coding.

5.3 Beyond the Paycheck: Non-Salary Benefits

When considering a job offer, don't fixate only on the salary number. The benefits package can add significant value (or cost savings) to your overall compensation. In fact, benefits often equate to an additional 10–20% (or more) of your compensation in value. A job with slightly lower salary but great benefits might actually leave you better off financially (and personally) than a higher-salary job with skimpy benefits. Let's review common non-salary benefits and why they matter:

Health Insurance: Nearly all employers offer a health plan. The key is how much of the premium they cover and the quality of the plan. Many hospitals and large groups cover about 80% of the premium for you (and often a slightly lower percentage for family members). For example, they might pay 80%, you pay 20% via payroll deduction. A richer benefit would be 90%+ of premiums paid by employer. Also look at deductibles, networks, etc. This can substantially affect your take-home – a plan where you pay $200/month vs $800/month is a difference of $7,200 a year. Full coverage of premiums is rare nowadays. Some employers also include dental and vision insurance. Tip: If you have a family, the portion of premium you must pay for dependents matters – e.g., some pay 70-80% for dependents, others less. Wellness programs are increasingly common; some places even discount your premium for healthy behaviors (e.g., attesting non-smoker, completing health screenings)

Retirement Plan: This is typically a 401(k) or 403(b) plan. The big factor is the employer match or contribution. A common offering might be "We match 100% of the first 3% of your salary you contribute, and 50% of the next 2%" (just an example). Some might do a flat 5% contribution even if you put nothing. Over years, this is huge. For instance, a 5% match on a $250k salary is $12,500 a year extra. Always contribute at least enough to get the full match – it's effectively part of your compensation. Check the vesting schedule: many plans vest immediately or after 1 year, but some may require say 3-5 years of service before the employer contributions are fully yours. If you leave earlier, you might forfeit some unvested match. Academic or government jobs might offer a pension (less common now) or 457(b) plans too.

Student Loan Repayment: With many physicians carrying hefty loans, some employers, especially in rural or underserved areas, offer loan repayment assistance. This can range widely – e.g., $50k over 2 years, or even $100k+ spread over several years, often tied to a commitment of service. Beware the strings attached: Usually, if you leave before the agreed time, you must pay back the loan money (a clawback). Often these programs require a 3-5 year commitment. Loan repayment is more common in hard-to-recruit areas (rural) and primary care. The recent ranges reported are quite broad – from $10,000 up to $200,000 depending on specialty and location. Importantly, loan repayment from an employer is typically taxable income (unless it's through a federal program like NHSC). Consider that in evaluating its worth. But it can be immensely helpful in knocking down debt.

Signing Bonus: Many jobs, particularly in high-need specialties or locations, offer a sign-on bonus. This is a one-time sum to entice you to join –

often ranging from $10k to $50k for many specialties, though some reports show ranges even up to $100k+ for in-demand fields. Crucial: Almost all sign-on bonuses require you to pay it back (often prorated) if you leave before a certain time, typically 2–3 years. For example, a $30k bonus might forgive 1/3 each year over 3 years; leave after 1 year and you owe $20k back. Treat a sign-on bonus as "earned over time." Also, know if it's paid upfront (common) or in installments. It will be taxed (so $30k might only net ~$20k after withholdings initially, and then if you have to repay, that's another tax complexity). Despite those caveats, bonuses are common and can help with transition costs or simply boost your starting bank balance. Just don't make the mistake of spending it all if there's a chance you might leave early.

Relocation Allowance: Moving for a new job can easily cost several thousand dollars (moving company, travel, temporary housing). Many employers offer a relocation stipend or reimbursement, often in the ballpark of $5,000 to $15,000. Some will pay the movers directly or reimburse your receipts, others just cut a flat check. Note: Due to tax law changes, as of now relocation reimbursement is taxable to you. So if they give $10k, you'll owe income tax on that as if it were bonus income. (In the past it was tax-free, not anymore.) Still, a good perk. Often if you leave very early, a portion may need to be paid back (similar to sign-on). Clarify if that's the case. Use relocation assistance to cover legitimate costs (house-hunting trips, movers, closing costs, etc. – see if there are limits on what's covered).

CME Allowance: Continuing Medical Education funds help cover costs of your ongoing training – e.g., conference fees, travel, board review courses, medical journals, online courses, etc. A typical CME allowance might be ~$3,000 to $5,000 per year, often with up to one week of paid time off for CME in addition to your regular vacation. This is a nice benefit, as it essentially covers your licensure, required education, and professional development. When comparing jobs, note both the dollar amount and whether they give dedicated CME days off (and if those days count against your vacation or not). Some places might offer fewer dollars but more time, or vice versa. If you plan to attend international conferences or expensive board prep, a higher CME budget is valuable. Also check if unused CME funds can roll over to the next year (some do, some don't).

Malpractice Insurance: This is such a big topic it has its own chapter, but suffice to say it's a necessary benefit. Most employers pay your malpractice premium. The type of policy (occurrence or claims-made) and whether tail is covered can significantly affect you if you leave. Always determine if the employer-provided malpractice includes tail coverage or not – more on this later. Disability and Life Insurance: Many employers provide a basic life insurance policy (often equal to 1× your annual salary at no cost). Some offer options to buy more at group rates. Similarly, long-term disability insurance is commonly offered – for example, a policy covering 60% of your salary if you become disabled. Employer LTD is usually inexpensive or free for you, but check if benefits would be taxable (if the employer pays the premium, any payout is taxable to you versus if you pay, the benefit would be tax-free). Some physicians still buy their own supplemental disability policy for stronger coverage, but getting the free/cheap employer one is a must. These benefits aren't flashy but are important safety nets.

Paid Time Off (Vacation/Sick Leave): PTO can vary widely. A typical range for physicians might be 4–6 weeks of total paid leave (including vacation and CME). Some jobs separate vacation, sick, CME days; others give a lump sum of PTO. While not "money" per se, time off is a valuable part of your compensation package and crucial for burnout prevention. Also ask about unpaid leave policies, parental leave, etc. In recent trends, organizations have become more explicit about how much time off you get and usually do not allow "banking" or payout of unused days. Make sure the offered time off meets your needs (e.g., if you have family far away, will you have enough days to visit them?).

Other perks: These might include moving assistance (covered above), academic funds if in academia, licensing/DEA fee reimbursement, professional society dues, cell phone or car allowances in some cases, wellness benefits (gym membership reimbursement, etc.), or even tuition assistance for your kids (rare, but some large systems have such perks). One increasingly common benefit is access to employee wellness programs or burnout resources – while not directly financial, they can improve quality of life and sometimes even lower your insurance premium if you participate. As you compare job offers, consider the totality of benefits. One offer might have a $10k higher salary, but if the other offers $30k of extra value in retirement contributions, loan repayment, and insurance, the latter is actually richer.

A wise approach is to literally add up the annual $value of each benefit: e.g., $employer pays for health premiums + $401k match + $CME + etc., and add to base salary to get a true comparison. An example given by an expert: one plan with a 5% 401k match vs another with none could mean a difference of tens of thousands over years.

Also weigh which benefits matter more to you personally. If you have huge loans, an employer paying $20k/year toward them might be worth more to you than one offering a slightly higher base salary but no loan help. If you have a family, good health insurance and ample PTO might take priority. In summary, benefits are a significant part of your compensation – don't overlook them. They can provide financial gains (or prevent losses) that add to your bottom line and improve your quality of life. Employers know that benefits are a retention tool, so good ones will often structure them to encourage you to stay (vesting schedules, multi-year bonuses, etc.). Understand the fine print (e.g., clawbacks on bonus/relocation, vesting periods) so you aren't caught by surprise. A well-rounded benefits package is a sign of a supportive employer and can make your transition into practice much smoother.

5.4 Call Pay and Valuing Your Time on Call

"Taking call" – be it hospital nights, weekends, or backup call – is a reality in many specialties. How your call duties are handled and compensated is a key aspect of your job. Call can range from light phone availability to intense in-hospital shifts, so it's important to clarify expectations and understand if there is additional pay for it.

What is Call and Why It Matters

Call generally means you're the designated physician to handle emergencies or inpatient needs during off-hours (nights, weekends, holidays) for a practice or hospital. The intensity varies:

Light call: e.g., a primary care doctor taking phone calls for their practice's patients after hours, which may be infrequent.

Heavy call: e.g., a trauma surgeon covering an ER, requiring immediate availability and likely hospital presence.

In-house vs. home call: Some specialties (anesthesia, OB, surgery) might require you to stay in the hospital (in-house call) ready to respond. Others allow you to be at home and only come in if needed (home call). In-house call is more disruptive (and often more likely to be paid separately).

For new physicians, call is often a point of negotiation. Ask upfront: How often will I be on call? What does call entail? Is there compensation for call?

Call Frequency and Distribution

Call responsibilities should be clearly spelled out in your contract or offer: * Is it a fixed rotation (like 1 in 4 nights)? Does it change as more people are hired? * Are weekends handled separately from weekdays? * If multiple sites, which ones will you cover on call? * Avoid vague language like "participate in call as needed." Ideally, it should say something like "physician will take call no more than X nights per month and X weekends per quarter, shared equally among Y physicians." Contracts should strive for an equitable call schedule. Watch out for situations where senior partners opt out of call, dumping more on junior docs – if such policies exist, understand them and ensure it's tolerable.

If call is expected as part of the job and not separately paid, make sure the overall compensation accounts for that. For instance, a hospitalist working 7-on/7-off might have night shifts as part of the schedule but no extra pay for them – that's normal because the salary is set with those nights in mind. But if you're, say, a neurologist taking stroke call for the ER on top of clinic, some places might pay for that.

Call Pay – How is it Calculated?

Call pay is far from uniform. Many hospitals have started paying stipends for on-call coverage, especially for specialties where call is burdensome or where they're required to have someone available (e.g., general surgery, ortho, cardiology in some areas). Here are common structures for call compensation:

Daily stipend: e.g., "$500 per weekday night of call, $1000 for a 24-hour weekend day." This is very common. You get paid a flat amount for carrying the pager whether you're called or not.

Hourly rate for call: Less common, but some places might pay per hour especially for in-house call. E.g., $100/hour for each hour on site after hours.

Pay per service while on call: Some arrangements give an on-call stipend plus additional pay if you have to come in for a case (like $X per surgery).

No additional pay (built-in): Many employed physicians simply have call as part of their job with no separate pay. Often true in primary care groups, some surgical practices, etc., especially if call volume is low or benefits the practice through downstream revenue.

Comp time: Instead of money, some practices give a post-call day off or additional PTO to compensate for heavy call duty.

In discussions among physicians, call pay can vary widely. Surveys show ranges like $200–$300 per weekday night for some specialties, and $500–$2000+ for a 24-hour weekend for others. Procedural specialties often report higher stipends. For example, anesthesiologists might get a different rate if they're called in to do a case versus just being available. Some internal medicine subspecialties might only get ~$200 for a weekend of phone availability. It truly runs the gamut. In one survey, call compensation for various fields ranged from a few hundred to over a thousand dollars per shift, and some physicians reported an annual call pay of tens of thousands if call is frequent. However, many got nothing extra if call was considered part of salary. So, know what's typical in your field and region.

Negotiating Call and Its Value

If the job involves a lot of call, you have a couple of negotiation angles:

Ask if call pay is offered or possible. If the initial offer doesn't mention it and you know peers in your specialty often get stipends, you can raise the question: "Is there compensation for extended call duties or particularly burdensome call?" The worst they say is no, but at least you open the discussion. Some employers might then sweeten the base salary to account for heavy call if they don't explicitly pay per call.

Limit call in contract: If you're concerned about excessive call, consider negotiating a cap. For instance, "no more than 7 on-call days per month" in the contract. Also ensure any language about sharing call is fair (e.g., if the group grows and you're still taking same frequency, that's okay, but if colleagues drop out, do you suddenly take every other night? There should be a plan).

Unpaid call but with subsequent benefits: If there's no pay, maybe negotiate post-call mornings off or the Monday after a weekend off, etc., to balance the workload. Some contracts allow for a "post-call day off" especially after intense weekends – if not automatically given, you can ask for it.

Also consider the burden of call: Is it home call where you sleep most nights or intense call with frequent sleep interruptions? Your stamina and life balance matter. If a job has brutal call expectations, even a high salary might not be worth the stress long-term.

On the flip side, if a job has no call at all, that's a lifestyle boost which might justify a slightly lower salary compared to another job where you're up all night every fourth night.

A Special Note on Compliance and "Fair Market" Call Pay

Why do some hospitals pay for call and others not? Often it depends on need and fairness. Surgical and specialty coverage for ERs is mandated (EMTALA requires hospitals to have on-call specialists). Many hospitals now pay stipends to secure that coverage, especially if specialists might otherwise opt out. However, any such payments have to be within fair market value (due to Stark Law / Anti-kickback regulations). Hospitals can't excessively pay for call as a kickback. They often rely on market surveys to set rates.

This is more a background issue, but if you're negotiating with a hospital for call pay, know that they will frame it as an FMV-based stipend.

Large discrepancies in call pay offers often come down to how desperate the hospital is and what's standard in that area.

Restricted vs. unrestricted call: If you must stay in-house (restricted), that usually warrants pay or a different structure (like shift pay). If it's unrestricted (home call), pay might be lower or none, depending on frequency of call-ins. Multiple facilities: If you cover more than one hospital on a single call shift, that's more work – sometimes they pay extra for multi-hospital coverage, or have separate pay from each (if, say, two hospitals both want you on call). Clarify this scenario if it exists.

Time Valuation: Your Time is Money

One way to look at call is by valuing your time. If you're on call without extra pay, effectively your salary covers those hours too. For instance, if you make $250k and you cover an extra 500 hours per year on call (just an example), that's 500 more hours of work for "free," lowering your effective hourly rate. Of course, you might not be actively working all those hours, but it's time you can't fully relax or leave town.

When negotiating, if they can't budge on salary or call pay, you might negotiate something like additional PTO or a lighter regular schedule in exchange for heavy call. Example: a cardiologist might accept an every 4th night call schedule if their clinic template is lighter the day after call. Some contracts explicitly state that if you get called in past midnight, you can start late or have a lighter load the next day.

Don't forget about burnout – frequent call can erode your well-being. If a job has extremely frequent call (like 1 in 2 or 1 in 3 for a demanding specialty), ask about their plans to recruit more help or mitigate burnout. Sometimes a high call burden is tolerable for a short term (a year or two) if the plan is to hire more physicians, but get that sense from them. In summary, call duties are an important part of your working life and should be discussed just as salary is. Make sure you understand: * Frequency and type of call expected. * Compensation or lack thereof for that call. * Impact on your schedule (do you still work full clinic day post-call?). * Any options to adjust these terms in the future (for example, if you develop health issues or life changes that make call difficult, can the group accommodate that down the line? Some groups let older physicians taper off call at a certain age).

If call is compensated, it can be a nice boost to income. If it's not, at least ensure the base pay is generous enough to reflect it. As one physician contract expert advised, "one thing to watch out for is disproportionate call responsibilities – ideally call duty is shared evenly". If you see language or patterns that suggest you'll be handling more than your share, address it before signing. Your personal time has value, and a good employer will acknowledge that either in pay or in policies.

5.5 Malpractice Insurance: Protecting Your Practice and Peace of Mind

One of the most important (and expensive) pieces of your professional puzzle is malpractice insurance. In almost all employed situations, the employer will provide and pay for your malpractice coverage – but you need to understand what type of policy it is, and what happens when you leave that job. A malpractice lawsuit can arise years after the care was provided, so the coverage details matter greatly. Let's break down key terms: occurrence vs. claims-made policies, tail coverage, policy limits, and cost.

Occurrence vs. Claims-Made Policies

These are two fundamentally different types of malpractice insurance:

Occurrence Policy: Covers any incident that occurred during the policy period, regardless of when the claim is filed. If you had an occurrence policy from 2023-2025 at Hospital A, and then you left, any claim for something that happened in 2024 would still be covered by that policy even if the claim comes in 2026 (after you've left). It's like permanent coverage for those years.

Claims-Made Policy: Covers you only if the claim is made while the policy is active (and the incident also happened after the policy's retroactive start date). If you leave a job with a claims-made policy, once the policy ends, you are no longer covered for claims that come in later, even if the incident happened while you were working there. Unless – you purchase an extension called "tail coverage."

In practical terms, occurrence is the gold standard (no tail needed) but is more expensive. Claims-made is cheaper initially but requires tail later. Most physicians (97% of new physicians, per one source) are offered claims-made coverage by employers. Occurrence policies are less common nowadays due to higher cost, though some hospitals or group practices may still have them. Why this matters to you: If you have a claims-made policy, when you leave the job or the policy is terminated, you must ensure coverage for any future claims from your time there. That's where tail coverage comes in.

Tail Coverage (Extended Reporting Endorsement)

Tail coverage is a supplemental policy you buy (usually a one-time purchase) when a claims-made policy ends, to cover any claims that arise after the end date for incidents that occurred while you were insured. In other words, tail picks up where your claims-made left off, covering the "tail" of exposure after you leave. Important points: Tail coverage can be quite expensive – often 1.5 to 2 times the annual premium for the policy (as a one-time cost) is a commonly cited estimate. For high-risk specialties, that can be a lot of money (e.g., if annual premium was $20k, tail might cost $30-40k).

Sometimes, instead of tail, a physician's new employer can purchase "nose" coverage (prior acts coverage) to cover their past acts. But many new employers, especially if you're just out of training, don't need to do that yet since you have no prior acts. Nose is more for when you switch jobs and the new insurer covers your tail by extending their policy retroactively.

The contract should specify who is responsible for tail if you leave. This is *HUGE*. Some employers will pay your tail as part of the deal (especially if they terminate you without cause, or after you complete a contract term). Others explicitly put it on the physician to buy tail if they leave. Tail can be negotiated – for example, if they won't budge on tail, perhaps you negotiate a higher signing bonus to help cover it when time comes.

If you have an occurrence policy, you do not need a tail. That's a perk of occurrence.

Many jobs handle it like this: if you leave after the contract term, you pay tail; but if they sell the practice or change carriers, they provide tail; or if they terminate you without cause, maybe they'll split tail cost. It varies. But roughly half the time the new practice might cover tail as a perk to recruit you, or the old practice might cover it to protect themselves. It's a negotiable item. Don't be afraid to ask "What about tail coverage – who covers it if I were to leave?"

Example scenario: You start your first job with a claims-made policy. After 3 years, you decide to move to another state. Your current contract says you must buy tail. You get a quote from the insurer: it's $50,000 (because you're in a high-risk field). If you weren't expecting that, it's a nasty surprise. Some physicians have felt "trapped" in jobs because tail was too pricey to leave easily. That's why clarifying this upfront is vital.

Policy Limits

Malpractice policies have coverage limits, often expressed per incident/aggregate. A typical standard for physicians is $1 million / $3 million – meaning up to $1 million coverage per claim, and $3 million total per policy year for all claims. Some hospitals or states might require different limits (e.g., 2M/4M, or 500k/1M in some places with patient compensation funds). For most private practice and hospital jobs, $1M/$3M is common and usually sufficient. If you do very high-risk work (like neurosurgery in a very litigious area), sometimes higher limits are offered. Interestingly, extremely high limits can make you a bigger "target" in a lawsuit (plaintiffs know the money is there), but as an individual physician, you often don't get to choose – the employer sets the group policy limits.

Key for you is simply to check that the coverage meets at least the local standard minimum. If you moonlight or do any work outside your employer, know that your employer's malpractice likely only covers your work for them. For any side gigs, you may need separate coverage or a rider.

Malpractice Insurance Cost (and why it matters to you even if not paying it)

Malpractice premiums vary immensely by specialty and location. Some illustrative figures: A general internist or family physician might have an annual premium around $8k–$15k (varies by state; was about $12.5k median in 2008 for IM, relatively stable since, maybe a bit higher now). A general surgeon might pay $30k–$50k a year in many states.

High-risk specialties like OB/GYN, neurosurgery can see premiums $80k, $100k, even upwards of $150k/year in high-litigation areas. In certain places, neurosurgeons faced $200–300k yearly premiums (e.g., some counties in New York, Florida).

Emergency medicine, ortho, anesthesiology, etc., fall somewhere in between, maybe $20k–$60k range depending on region.

These costs typically are borne by the employer if you're employed. If you join a small practice as a partner or independent contractor, you might be paying it yourself, so then it's crucial to know. Even as an employee, it's good to know the cost because if an employer is covering an especially expensive premium for you, they might offset it with slightly lower salary. For instance, an OB job in a state with very high premiums might offer lower salary than one in a tort-reform state, because the employer's overhead is higher.

One more thing: malpractice tail cost on departure – remember that if tail is on you, its price is a function of the premium. So high-premium specialty = very high tail cost. That's why many contracts for, say, neurosurgery will try to negotiate occurrence coverage or an employer-paid tail, because otherwise it's a big burden on the doc.

Occurrence vs Claims-Made Recap with Example

Dr. Alice and Dr. Bob both finished residency in 2025 and go to work:

Alice's job provides occurrence coverage. In 2025, she treats a patient. In 2028, after Alice has moved on, that patient files a lawsuit. Alice is covered, because it occurred in 2025 when she had coverage with that employer. No further action needed from Alice.

Bob's job provides claims-made. In 2025 he treats a patient. He leaves in 2027. In 2028 the patient files a suit. Bob's 2025–27 policy was claims-made and is no longer active in 2028. Bob only has coverage in 2028 if he bought a tail when he left in 2027. If he did, the tail now covers the 2028 claim. If he didn't, uh-oh – he's essentially uninsured for that incident and could be personally liable.

Thus, with claims-made, tail is not optional – it's a necessity (one way or another) to protect yourself. Many new physicians ensure their contract either includes employer-paid tail or plan financially for tail if they leave. If a new employer really wants you, sometimes they'll cover your tail from the old job – but that's often in recruitment scenarios for experienced docs, not first jobs.

Additional Malpractice Considerations

Defense and limits: Make sure the policy covers legal defense costs outside the liability limits or clarify if they erode the limits. Some cheaper policies might have defense costs count against the limit (so a big legal defense could use up some of the $1M coverage). Ideally, you want "$1M plus defense." Most standard policies do cover defense in addition.

Consent to settle: Does the policy require your consent to settle a claim? Many employer policies might not give individual doctors full say (the hospital might settle a case even if you want to fight). Just be aware of the policy's terms. Some states give physicians the right to be consulted or consent.

Tail upon retirement: Some contracts/insurance have a provision that if you retire or die, tail is forgiven or purchased by the policy. If you plan to retire from that employer, ask if they have a tail provision for that scenario.

Claims history: As you practice, any claims made will become part of your record. Even if dismissed, you'll have to disclose that on credentialing forms. Good insurance and legal defense will help manage claims. But hopefully you won't face any early in your career.

The bottom line: When you review a job offer or contract, find the section on malpractice insurance. Verify: * The type of coverage (claims-made vs occurrence). * The policy limits (e.g., $1M/$3M standard). * Who pays for tail if applicable.

If it's not explicitly in the contract, ask in writing for clarification. It's that important. A good employer should be transparent about this. One ACP advice piece put it bluntly: understanding these differences can mean the difference between adequate protection vs. personal financial ruin if something goes wrong. That might sound dramatic, but malpractice claims can be very costly, and you want to be sure your assets are shielded by proper coverage.

Luckily, for most employed positions, malpractice is covered and routine. Just ensure you don't accidentally go bare (uninsured) during job transitions, and factor in tail coverage plans if you leave. With this knowledge, you can sign your contract with peace of mind that you're protected while caring for patients.

Chapter 6

Contracts

Your physician employment contract is a legal document defining your work life – it deserves careful attention. While contracts can be long and full of legal jargon, understanding key clauses and negotiating where appropriate can save you from headaches later. Remember, everything is negotiable to some extent, though there may be limits. Don't be shy about advocating for yourself – approach it professionally, not combatively. This section will highlight key contract clauses, offer negotiation strategies, flag red flags, and emphasize the importance of a legal review.

6.1 Key Contract Clauses to Understand

Not every contract is the same, but most will cover similar core areas. Here are the big ones to look for:

Duties and Scope of Work: What exactly is expected of you? It should outline your specialty, work site(s), clinical duties, any administrative roles, teaching, etc. Beware of very vague language. If you're joining as a general surgeon but the contract says "physician will perform clinical duties as assigned by employer," that's too open-ended. Ideally, it specifies clinic hours vs hospital rounds, call responsibilities (or references a schedule), and any outreach clinics, etc. If the contract doesn't list it, ask for clarification. For instance, if they expect you to supervise mid-levels or cover an urgent care occasionally, that should be mentioned. Hours and schedule should be at least broadly defined – e.g., "full-time defined as 40 hours per week of patient care on average, with schedule set by mutual agreement." If call coverage isn't detailed here, ensure it's somewhere (perhaps in a separate call pay addendum or so). Lack of specifics on duties and hours is a red flag – it can lead to you being overworked unexpectedly.

Compensation and Bonus Structure: This is obviously crucial. Ensure the contract clearly states your base salary and any incentive formula (and timeline for recalculation if applicable). If RVU-based, the rate per RVU and any thresholds should be spelled out. If bonus is based on "quality metrics," the actual metrics or an appendix describing them should be included. Ask for examples of how the compensation formula works in practice. If the formula is extremely complex or unclear, that's a bad sign. You should be able to look at the contract and understand how you get paid (maybe not to the dollar, but at least the method) – "muddled compensation formula" is a common contract pitfall. Clarity is key: if something like a productivity bonus is mentioned but not quantified, ask for clarification or insertion of the specifics.

Term and Termination: How long does the contract last and how can it end? Many physician contracts are either at-will or for a term (like 1-3 years) but with clauses to end early. Key parts: * **Without cause termination:** Most contracts allow either party to terminate without cause with notice (e.g., 60-90 days' notice). This means either you or the employer can walk away for any reason or no reason. Check the notice period – you want enough time to find a new job if they cut you loose (90 or 120 days notice is better than 30). Also importantly, see if the employer has any provision to terminate you sooner if you give notice (some have a clause to "accelerate termination" which basically means if you resign with 90 days notice, they reserve the right to make your last day sooner – potentially leaving you without pay for part of your notice). That's a red flag to watch for; you'd want to negotiate that out or at least ensure you'd still get compensated for the notice period. * **For cause termination:** The contract will list reasons you can be fired for cause (e.g., losing your license, committing a crime, breaching the contract, etc.). Ensure it's reasonably specific and ideally that it requires notice and a chance to cure minor issues. Vague for-cause reasons like "conduct unbecoming" or "damage to reputation" are subjective and concerning. If they exist, one might negotiate adding language like "reasonably determined in good faith by employer" or have an opportunity to address issues.

Contract term length & renewal: Some automatically renew each year unless notice given, others expire unless renewed. Just note what it is and if it matters for things like bonus timing or partnership consideration. Non-Compete (Restrictive Covenant): Many contracts have a clause restricting where you can work for a period after leaving. For example, "Physician shall not practice within 10 miles of Employer's primary office or any site Physician provided services for 1 year after termination." Non-competes are common but must be reasonable in scope, duration, and geographic area. Overly broad noncompetes are a red flag. If it's, say, 50 miles for 3 years covering every facility of a huge health system, that could effectively force you to move away to work – that's onerous. Some tips: * Try to narrow it: e.g., only apply to the specific clinic/hospital you worked at, not every affiliate site; or reduce the radius (is 5 miles enough instead of 15? Especially in urban vs rural context, what's reasonable differs). * Ensure it doesn't apply if they terminate you without cause. If you get fired or laid off, it's extra harsh to also stop you from working nearby. One expert suggests making sure a restrictive covenant does not apply in a termination without cause scenario. * Some states don't enforce physician non-competes, but many do with limits. Regardless, negotiate as if it will be enforced. * Non-solicitation of patients is slightly different (usually you agree not to actively lure patients away, which is more acceptable and often included). But some contracts go further, barring you from even seeing any former patients for a period – that can impinge on patient rights and is often overly broad (and may not hold up legally).

Compensation for Tail / Malpractice Clause: As discussed in the previous chapter, check what the contract says about malpractice coverage and tail. Ideally: "Employer shall maintain professional liability insurance of at least X limits, on a [claims-made/occurrence] basis. If claims-made, Employer [will / will not] purchase tail coverage." If it says you must buy tail, that's something to be aware of and possibly negotiate if it's a deal-breaker (maybe they could cover tail if you work a certain number of years, etc.).

Benefits Clause: It might briefly say "Physician is eligible for standard hospital benefits as per hospital policy." Not super specific, but ensure major promised things (loan repayment, etc.) are either in contract or offer letter. Often benefits are in a separate handbook, but anything really important to you – like a signing bonus or specific stipend – should be in writing either in the contract or an addendum.

Productivity expectations and support: If your pay or future salary increases depend on productivity, it's fair to ask for assurances about how things like patient volume will be managed. For instance, if you're paid on RVUs but they severely limit your clinic slots or there aren't enough referrals, that's problematic. Some contracts (or at least discussions) might address support staff provided, marketing support, etc. This isn't always in writing, but you can at least ask in negotiations how they'll help you succeed.

Partnership or Track (if applicable): In private practices, the contract might outline if/when you can become a partner. E.g., "after 2 years, eligible to purchase shares" with some formula. Or it may be silent, in which case discuss verbally and perhaps get a mention in an offer letter. Know that partnership details are often separate agreements later, but you want some sense of the timeline and buy-in cost. If an employer dangles partnership but won't put anything about it in writing at all, be cautious.

Assignment Clause: This allows the employer to assign the contract to another entity. For example, if the practice is sold, they can transfer your contract to the new owner. This is common. However, as AMA warns, it can be surprising if you're suddenly working for a different employer without consent. Not usually negotiable (they'll keep it), but be aware it exists.

Dispute Resolution: Some contracts require arbitration or mediation instead of court for disputes. Arbitration clauses mean you waive right to trial. It's not necessarily bad, but check if it's one-sided. Also check if there's an attorneys' fees clause (often if either party has to enforce the contract, the prevailing party gets fees covered). That can cut both ways.

Indemnification: Occasionally, contracts have an indemnity clause where you agree to reimburse the employer for certain losses (e.g., if you do something outside scope). These are usually not prominent in physician contracts, but keep an eye out. You ideally don't want to personally indemnify a big health system for random things. Restrictive Covenants beyond non-compete: Like non-solicitation of employees (you won't poach staff if you leave) – fairly standard. Just ensure reasonable time frame (1-2 years typically).

Moonlighting/Outside Work: Does the contract bar you from doing any work outside the employer? Many will say you need written permission to "engage in other medical practice or employment." If you plan to moonlight, mention it and get permission (in writing). If you write or do consulting, clarify what's allowed.

Buyout Clauses: If there's a non-compete, sometimes there's an option to buy it out (like paying a certain amount to void it). If you see that, note the cost and consider negotiating it down if it's exorbitant.

It's a lot, but focus on the clauses that impact your day-to-day life and ability to leave if needed (those are usually compensation, termination, call, non-compete, and malpractice).

6.2 Negotiation Strategies for Physicians

Negotiating a contract can be uncomfortable for physicians not used to it. But remember, employers expect some negotiation – you're a highly skilled professional. Approach it collegially: "I'm very excited about the offer. I did have a few questions and a couple of requests I was hoping we could discuss." Here are tips:

Prioritize your asks: Determine what matters most (salary, call, location, tail coverage, etc.). Don't present a laundry list of 20 changes. Focus on a few key points. As one article advises, make a list of must-haves vs nice-to-haves. That way, you can concede smaller points while holding ground on the important ones.

Do your homework: Know the typical salary range and benefits for your specialty in that region. Use resources (MGMA data if available, or even speaking with recent grads, recruiters, etc.). This gives you confidence in negotiations. If you know the offer is below median, you can politely point that out and express that you were expecting something closer to $X given the market. Also, if relocating, mention cost of living differences if relevant.

Be reasonable and professional: You don't want to come off as adversarial. Phrase things positively. For example, instead of "This non-compete is unacceptable," say "I have some concern about the breadth of the non-compete. Is there flexibility to narrow the radius? I'd like to ensure it's fair in case things don't work out, while still protecting the practice's interests." This shows you understand their side too.

Get everything in writing: If they agree to something verbally, it must be reflected in the contract or an amendment. A classic mistake is taking someone's word that "we never enforce that clause" or "we will cover that expense for you" without it being written. As a mentor might say: If it's not in writing, it didn't happen. Always have changes made in the contract text or at least in a signed offer letter addendum.

Use advisors as needed: Consider hiring an attorney experienced in physician contracts (more on that in a moment). Also, talk to mentors or colleagues about what's typical. If joining a hospital, perhaps the hospital's physician liaison can clarify things. Just be mindful of advice – ensure advisors know local norms. Leverage but don't bluff too hard: If you have another offer or interest, it can sometimes help to mention it (tactfully) to show you have options. But be careful about bluffing something that's not true or issuing ultimatums unless you're prepared to walk. Negotiation is a give-and-take, and you want to preserve a good relationship for when you start the job.

Ask questions: Sometimes phrasing a negotiation point as a question yields results. "Is the salary negotiable at all?" or "What flexibility is there on the tail coverage responsibility?" This invites them to explain or improve terms without a direct demand. It also signals that you know to ask – which *"demonstrates you've done your homework and speaks well of you professionally," as the AMA notes. Indeed, most employers expect some questions; asking them shows diligence, not greed.

If the employer is very resistant to reasonable changes, or if they are pressuring you to sign quickly without time to review, those are warning signs. One expert said if you feel extremely uncomfortable or disrespected in negotiation, that's a bad omen for working there. You want an employer who respects that you carefully review contracts.

6.3   Red Flags to Watch Out For

Some contract issues are so concerning that they merit careful consideration or walking away if not rectified. We've touched on many, but here's a summary of common red flags:

Overly broad non-compete: For instance, covering a huge radius or multiple counties, especially if you'd have to uproot your life to get around it. Or applying even if they terminate you without cause. Non-competes should be no broader than necessary to protect legitimate business interests. If it feels punitive, try to modify it.

Unclear compensation formula or promises not in writing: If you can't decipher how your bonus works, or there are vague mentions of productivity without specifics. This lack of clarity is a bad sign. You don't want to find out later that the bonus was essentially unattainable. A muddled compensation formula is explicitly cited as a red flag – you deserve clarity on how you'll earn.

Disproportionate or unlimited call: If the contract doesn't specify call or says something like "will take call as needed," be careful. Also if you discover that several senior docs take no call so you'll be on every other night – not sustainable. "Disproportionate call responsibilities" were highlighted as something to avoid. Ideally put a limit or equal share requirement in the contract.

One-sided termination provisions: E.g., the employer can fire you with 30 days notice but you have to give 180 days notice. Or they can fire you immediately if you give notice (accelerating termination). Or termination for cause reasons that are entirely subjective ("if we think you're not a good fit"). You want fairness and some ability to remedy issues. If they refuse to adjust very unfair terms, red flag.

No mention of tail coverage on claims-made policy: If contract is silent, assume it's on you – but clarify. If they explicitly say you must buy tail and you know that could be a huge cost, that's a financial risk. Not necessarily a deal-breaker if salary accounts for it, but you need to weigh it.

Repayment obligations: Look for any clause that says if you leave before X years, you owe them money (like for recruiting costs, training, etc.). Repaying sign-on or relocation is normal if you leave early, but ensure it prorates (if you almost fulfilled the time, you shouldn't owe the full amount). If they have an out-sized penalty, that's concerning.

Inclusion of unattainable or unspecified performance expectations: For example, if contract says you will "maintain a practice of at least 5,000 patients" or generate X RVUs without the infrastructure to support that – be wary.

Employer can change terms unilaterally: Some contracts might say employer reserves the right to change compensation or duties at any time. That's scary. While some flexibility is needed in medicine, any major change should require mutual agreement or at least notice and a chance to exit if you don't agree.

No due process for peer review actions: If you're hospital-employed, check if there's any protection that you won't be terminated until after medical staff due process if there's an allegation affecting privileges. It's complex, but basically you want to know you can defend yourself in any quality accusation before job loss.

Pressure to sign quickly: If they say "We need this back in 48 hours or the offer is off," that's a bullying tactic. A reasonable employer gives you time to review and even consult a lawyer. If they are rushing, it could mean they're hiding something or will be difficult to deal with.

On the flip side, green flags are employers who are transparent, willing to discuss and explain contract terms, and perhaps have a standardized but fair contract they are proud of. Some large institutions won't negotiate every little clause due to policy, but they might still clarify things for you and make minor adjustments.

6.4 Legal Review: Yes, It's Worth It

While you can parse a lot on your own, it's often wise to have an experienced health care attorney review your contract. They know the legal fine print and what's common in your state. They can explain the implications and suggest changes. Many times, an attorney will mark up a few items that you can then discuss with the employer. Costs for contract review vary – some do a flat fee (ranging $300-$1000 typically) which is a worthy investment for something this important. The attorney can also spot any Stark Law or compliance issues, ensure the contract language aligns with what you were promised, and basically be your backstop.

Even if you don't hire a lawyer to negotiate for you, getting their advice is valuable. Then you, armed with that advice, can negotiate with the employer's representative (often a practice manager or HR or their lawyer).

Special case: If the contract is with a large academic center or hospital, it might be fairly standard and "not negotiable" in many areas. Still, have a lawyer review so you know what you're signing. They might catch something like the contract requiring arbitration in another state, etc.

Remember, a contract is there for when things don't go as planned. Everyone is happy at signing. It's if conflict or misunderstandings arise that the contract becomes crucial. That's why those seemingly minor clauses matter. In short, approach contract negotiation as a normal part of the hiring process. Don't be timid – asking questions and negotiating shows professionalism. Most employers won't pull an offer just because you asked for a few reasonable changes. They may say no to some, but that's part of the back-and-forth. And if something is truly non-negotiable, they'll tell you, and then you decide if it's a deal-breaker or not.

Once you and the employer reach agreement on terms, get the final contract version with all changes included and read it again to ensure everything is as agreed. Then you can sign with confidence, knowing you've done your due diligence to start your new job on solid footing.

Chapter 7

Long-Term Financial Security

When you're just starting out, retirement might seem a lifetime away. But the decisions you make now can set you up for long-term financial security (or headaches). Plus, retirement benefits are a significant part of your compensation. Let's go through the common retirement plan options you'll see in a job contract for physicians.

7.1 Retirement Plans

401(k) Plans: If you join a for-profit employer or private practice, they'll likely offer a 401(k). This is a retirement savings account where you can contribute pre-tax (and/or post-tax Roth, if offered) money each pay period. The big thing to look for is the employer match or contribution. For example, a typical match might be "100% of the first 3% you contribute, and 50% of the next 2%," meaning if you put in 5% of your salary, they contribute 4% (for a total of 9% going into your 401k). Always try to contribute at least enough to get the full match – that's part of your compensation! In 2025, you can contribute up to $22,500/year (limit goes up most years) of your own money, and if over 50, there's catch-up. Some physician employers might even contribute a certain percentage regardless of your contribution (like 3% safe harbor contribution or profit-sharing contributions at year-end). These plans are governed by ERISA, have vesting schedules sometimes (e.g. you only keep the match if you stay 3 years), so check the vesting period.

403(b) Plans: Nonprofit hospitals or academic institutions use 403(b) plans, which are basically the nonprofit cousin of the 401(k). They function almost identically in terms of contribution limits and tax treatment. So if you're at a university hospital or large nonprofit system, you'll likely have a 403(b). Ask about matching contributions here as well; many nonprofits also match or contribute to 403(b)s.

457(b) Deferred Compensation Plans: This is a less common one, but many large nonprofit health systems or government employers offer a 457(b) in addition to a 403(b). A 457(b) is a deferred comp plan that allows another set of contributions up to $22,500 (totally separate from the 401k/403b limit). So if you have both a 403(b) and a 457(b), you as a physician can sock away double the money (e.g. $22.5k into the 403b and $22.5k into the 457b). This is a huge perk for high earners wanting to turbocharge retirement savings. However, 457(b)s have quirks:

- Only public employers or nonprofits can offer them (private practices can't).
- The money technically is deferred compensation of the employer – which means unlike a 401k/403b, it's subject to the employer's creditors until it's paid to you. In other words, if the employer went bankrupt, 457(b) funds could be at risk. (Governmental 457s are a bit safer than nonprofit ones in this regard.)
- You typically can't roll a 457(b) into an IRA until you separate employment, and often you have to take the distribution (or roll it) when you leave that job.

That said, a 457(b) is a nice deal if you trust the stability of the employer – it's another tax-advantaged bucket. For example, some academic physicians maximize both 403(b) and 457(b) to really build a nest egg.

Pension Plans (Defined Benefit Plans): These are increasingly rare unicorns in medicine, but a few large institutions still have them (or a hybrid cash-balance pension). A defined benefit pension means the employer promises a certain benefit at retirement (like monthly income for life based on salary and years of service). Examples: The military and VA have pensions, some old-school hospitals or state systems do. A 2024 review found some top hospitals like Mayo Clinic, Cleveland Clinic, and certain big systems still offer pension plans for their physicians. If you land a job with a pension, appreciate how valuable that is – it's like a guaranteed income later. However, most new physicians won't see a pension unless in government service. More common now might be a cash balance plan in some private practices, which is a pension-like plan where the company contributes on your behalf to a pooled fund that grows and at retirement you get a lump sum or annuity. If your group has one, great – it's icing on the cake (and they will explain your "buy-in" etc. if it's a partnership thing).

What to do

- **Enroll ASAP:** Make sure you sign up for the retirement plan when you're eligible. Some plans start Day 1, others after 30 or 90 days, etc. Don't miss the window.
- **Contribute enough for the match:** That's free money. Think of it as part of your salary – if they match up to 5%, and you're not putting in 5%, you're leaving money on the table.
- **Consider Roth vs Traditional:** Some plans offer Roth 401k/403b option (you contribute post-tax, and then it grows tax-free, no tax on withdrawal in retirement). If you expect to be in a higher tax bracket now than retirement, traditional (pre-tax) might be better; if you're early career and think taxes might go up later, Roth could be great. Sometimes doing a mix is wise. This can get complex, so consider a financial advisor's input if needed.
- **Vesting:** Check how long until the employer contributions are fully yours. Common is 3-year cliff or 5-year graded vesting. If you leave before vested, you might forfeit some of those employer contributions (your contributions are always yours).
- **Retirement Plan options for partnerships:** If you're joining a private practice, see if they have a 401k or SEP-IRA or other plan. Smaller practices might do profit-sharing or have less structured plans. If none exists, that's something you may want to implement if you become a partner.

Big Picture

Saving for retirement might not feel urgent with your loans and new attending life, but starting early is incredibly powerful (hello, compounding interest). As one financial rule of thumb, aim to save at least 15-20% of your gross income for retirement/investments early in your career, and even more if you can. If you're heavy in debt payoff now, at least do enough to get matches and maybe ramp up savings after loans are gone. Automating through a 401k makes it much easier to build wealth in the background.

One more thing: some employers offer 457(f) plans or Supplemental Executive Retirement Plans (SERPs) for very high earners or leadership positions, which are beyond the scope of this chapter. Those are more like selective golden handcuffs for later.

To sum up, evaluate the retirement options in your job offer. A good plan with a strong match (or even better, a pension) significantly boosts the total compensation value. And by taking advantage of these plans, you'll thank yourself later when you have a solid retirement stash. Think of it as paying your "future self" – and with the help of employer money and tax breaks to boot.

7.2 Protecting Your Health: Health Insurance

Medicine might be your calling, but you're also a healthcare consumer yourself. Health insurance benefits are a core part of your job package, and it's important to ensure you and your family are well-covered. Let's break down what to look for in your new job's health insurance.

Types of Plans

Employers may offer a menu of plans:

PPO (Preferred Provider Organization): Usually higher premiums but more flexibility in choosing doctors and specialists without referrals. Good if you want choice or have specific doctors you want to see.

HMO (Health Maintenance Organization): Typically lower cost but you're more restricted to a network and often need referrals to see specialists.

High-Deductible Health Plan (HDHP) with HSA: Lower premiums, higher deductibles. Paired with a Health Savings Account (HSA) where you can set aside pre-tax money to pay for medical expenses. HSAs are great tax-wise (money in is tax-free, grows tax-free, and used for health expenses tax-free). But an HDHP means if you have a major medical issue, you'll pay more out-of-pocket until you hit the deductible.

POS or EPO Plans: Hybrids of HMO/PPO features; specifics vary.

Find out what exactly is offered. Many hospitals provide a few options (like an HDHP vs a PPO). If you have the option of an HSA-eligible plan and you're generally healthy, it can be financially savvy to take it and let that HSA grow (HSAs can even act as a secondary retirement account if unused).

Premiums and Cost Sharing

How much do you pay vs the employer? A lot of jobs fully cover the employee's premium and ask you to pay if you add family members. Others have a cost-share for any enrollee. For example, the plan might cost $600/month for you and your employer pays $500, you pay $100. If you add a spouse and kids, that might jump and your share might be a few hundred more. Those costs effectively reduce your take-home pay, so they are part of the compensation picture.

Deductibles, Copays, Out-of-Pocket Max

Examine the plan details:

Deductible: what you must pay each year before insurance really kicks in (except usually preventative care is covered 100%). An HDHP might have a $3k deductible; a PPO might have a $500 deductible.

Copays/Coinsurance: After deductible, you might pay a copay (like $30 per office visit) or coinsurance (like you pay 20%, insurance 80% for services).

Out-of-Pocket Maximum: The most you would pay in a year if you had a lot of medical bills. Important for worst-case scenario – e.g. an $6,000 max means once you've paid that, insurance covers 100% beyond that in the year.

Make sure you could handle the worst-case out-of-pocket in an emergency (that's also what emergency funds are for).

Network: Check if the network includes the medical groups and hospitals you prefer (funny enough, as a physician, you might care which hospital you'd want to be treated at). If you're staying in the same area as your training, you might want to keep your personal doctors – see if they accept the insurance. If not, you might have to switch or choose a different plan if available.

Start Date of Coverage: As mentioned earlier, ideally coverage starts when you start working. However, it's common that coverage might begin the first of the month after your start date (or after 30 days). For example, you start July 15, coverage begins Aug 1. If that's the case, you need to arrange a short-term plan or extend your residency insurance or COBRA for that half month. If it's 60 or 90 days delay (some places do 60 or 90 day waiting period), you definitely need interim coverage. Try to negotiate an earlier start if possible, because paying COBRA is expensive (often $600+ per month).

Family Considerations: If you have a family, examine the family coverage. Are spouse and kids covered with a manageable premium? Some employers impose a surcharge if your spouse could get their own insurance but opts onto yours. Also check maternity coverage details if you plan on having children – most group plans cover this fully, but out-of-pocket costs can vary.

Health Incentives: Some employers have wellness incentives – e.g. they lower your premium if you do a health screening, or contribute to your HSA if you complete an annual physical, etc. Small perks, but worth knowing.

Other Health Benefits

Many packages also include:

Dental Insurance: Usually optional and you pay a premium (often like

$30-50/month). Covers cleanings and part of costs for fillings, etc. If offered and you need dental work, it can be worth it.

Vision Insurance: Covers eye exams, glasses/contacts partially. Often cheap add-on like <$10/month.

These are not high-ticket items, but nice to have if you will use them.

Disability & Life: They're not health insurance, but they're part of the health/security net. Disability insurance is particularly important for protecting your earning capacity.

Flex Spending Accounts (FSAs): If not on an HSA plan, you might have access to an FSA for healthcare or dependent care. These let you set aside pre-tax dollars for medical or childcare expenses within the year. If offered, consider using them for known expenses (e.g. dependent care FSA if you pay for daycare – great tax saver).

If you have multiple plan choices, decide what matters: low premium vs low deductible, breadth of network vs cost, etc. As a physician, you might lean towards robust coverage (you know the system's ins and outs, and you want hassle-free care for your family).

COBRA

If you're leaving a residency or prior job mid-year and have a gap to new insurance, you can elect COBRA to continue your old coverage for up to 18 months. But you pay the full premium plus admin fee. Use it as a short-term bridge if needed. For longer gaps, look at ACA marketplace plans possibly.

In summary, don't just gloss over the health insurance section of your offer. It may be routine, but differences in coverage can amount to thousands of dollars and lots of peace of mind. Most likely, your new job's health plan will be solid, but double-check things like start date, family coverage, and any unusual cost-sharing. You want to hit the ground running medically covered – after all, you'll be telling patients to get their screenings and take care of their health, so make sure your own healthcare house is in order!

7.3   Planning for the Future: Financial Literacy

You've gone from resident scraping by on $60k to an attending making several times that overnight. It's tempting to shout "I'm rich!" and start living large. But hold up: This is the best time to get your financial life in order and set good habits. Let's talk budgeting, investing, and planning now that you have a "real" income.

Live Like a Resident (for a Bit): You may have heard this mantra. The idea is to not dramatically increase your lifestyle for the first few years as an attending. You're finally out of training – you deserve some lifestyle upgrades, sure. But if you can keep living relatively frugally for even 1-2 more years, you can use that extra income to wipe out debt and jump-start savings. For example, if you go from $60k to $250k, your monthly take-home might go from ~$4k to ~$12k. Instead of immediately finding ways to spend that extra $8k, imagine still living on maybe $6k and using $6k/month to kill loans or max out investments. In a couple years, you could be debt-free or have a huge nest egg. Then you have decades to enjoy the nicer things with far less financial stress.

Make a Budget (or at least a plan): Budgeting doesn't have to mean coupon-clipping drudgery. At its core it's deciding where your money will go each month. One simple rule is the 50/30/20 rule: 50% of take-home for needs, 30% for wants, 20% for savings/debt. As a high earner, you might aim for more like 30%+ to savings. In fact, one financial advisor suggests new attendings save about 30% of their income (25% for retirement, 5% for other goals). Start by listing your fixed expenses: rent/mortgage, utilities, insurance, loan payments, etc. Then decide an amount for flexible spending: dining, travel, etc. Importantly, decide how much to allocate to debt payoff and investing. Paying yourself first (into savings/investments) ensures it happens.

Emergency Fund:: If you don't already have one, build an emergency fund of at least 3-6 months' worth of living expenses. This money (kept in a savings account) is your cushion for unexpected events – job change, illness, big home/car repair. As an attending, if you're a sole breadwinner or have a big mortgage, maybe even 9-12 months' saved is prudent. This prevents small emergencies from turning into financial disasters or high-interest credit card debt.

Attack High-interest Debt: Many new docs have a mix of student loans, maybe a car loan, possibly credit card debt. Any debt with high interest (like credit cards) should be paid off ASAP, no question. For student loans, if you're not going for forgiveness, consider aggressive payoff of those above a certain rate or refinancing them. Some people prioritize loans, others invest at the same time – it can depend on interest rates (e.g., pay off a 7% loan, but maybe just pay minimum on a 2.5% refinanced loan and invest extra cash for higher returns). Emotionally, being debt-free feels great, so find your balance.

Investing 101

Now that you have more income, you should invest for long-term growth, not just save. We talked about retirement accounts in an earlier section

(401k/403b, etc.) – those are key. You should max out tax-advantaged accounts like your 401k/403b ($22.5k/year), backdoor Roth IRA if applicable (~$6,500/year), HSA if you have one ($3.8k single/$7.75k family). Those give tax benefits and grow over time. Beyond that, you might invest in a regular brokerage account. As for investing strategy:

For most docs, a simple diversified portfolio of index mutual funds or ETFs is ideal. Low-cost index funds (like those tracking the S&P 500, total stock market, international stock, and bonds) spread your money across many companies and are recommended by many financial experts.

You could consider a financial advisor, but be careful: choose fee-only fiduciary advisors, not salespeople who earn commissions on products. A good advisor can help create a plan and manage investments for a fee (typically 1% or less of assets per year, or a flat fee). But honestly, many physicians learn to DIY invest with a bit of reading (resources like White Coat Investor, etc. are geared to helping docs manage their money).

Avoid get-rich-quick schemes or exotic investments you don't understand. You'll likely get pitched on whole life insurance, dubious real estate deals, or the hot stock tip. Educate yourself before diving in.

Insurance Check

Financial planning includes having the right insurance. Make sure you have:

Term Life Insurance if anyone depends on your income (spouse, kids, maybe even to cover your loans or mortgage). Term life is cheap for young healthy people – get enough coverage (e.g. $1-5 million depending on need) for a term that covers until kids are grown or loans are paid.

Own-Occupation Disability Insurance: Yes, your job likely provides LTD group coverage, but an individual policy can supplement it to, say, replace 60-70% of your income, and importantly, define disability as inability to work in your specialty. That means if you can't be a surgeon due to injury, it pays, even if you could technically do another job. This protects your biggest asset: your future earning potential.

Umbrella liability insurance (an add-on to home/auto) can also protect you from non-work liability (like someone getting hurt on your property).

Avoid Lifestyle Creep (within reason)

By all means, treat yourself to something nice when you start earning (you deserve a reliable car instead of that beater, or a nice vacation after years of no time off). But try to avoid locking yourself into massive new monthly obligations all at once. The classic pitfalls: buying a house that's too expensive right away, or leasing a fancy car, or generally inflating expenses to match the new income. A good approach is to *incrementally* increase lifestyle. For example, maybe rent a nicer place but not the penthouse, or buy a modest home you can easily afford rather than a McMansion. Remember, attending income can be volatile too (changes in practices, burnout, etc.), so don't overspend assuming it'll always be rosy.

Set Goals

Think about what you want in 5, 10, 20 years. Home purchase? College fund for kids? Starting a business? Retirement at 60? Your financial plan (budgeting and investing) should align with these. If buying a home in a few years is a goal, start saving for a down payment now. If you have kids, consider starting a 529 college savings plan once they're born.

Educate Yourself

You spent years learning medicine; spend at least a few hours learning personal finance basics. It will pay huge dividends (pun intended). Books like *The White Coat Investor*, *Physician Finance 101*, or even free blogs and forums can teach you about taxes, asset protection, and smart investing. Knowledge helps you avoid being taken advantage of by bad actors (there are those who prey on doctors financially). As you earn more, also be mindful of tax planning – maybe get a CPA if your situation warrants.

The easiest way to stick to a financial plan is automation. Set up automatic contributions to savings and investment accounts every month. If it's out of sight, it's out of mind and you won't be tempted to spend it. For instance, auto-transfer $2000 each month to a brokerage or have $X go to loans directly. That way you pay yourself (and your future) first, then live on the rest.

In summary, financial literacy is part of being a successful physician in the long run. You don't have to become a Wall Street guru, but understanding the basics of budgeting, debt, and investing will ensure your hard-earned money actually works for you. You have a golden opportunity in your first attending years to set the foundation: you're finally earning well – use that to secure your future, not just upgrade your present. Future you will be very grateful.

Chapter 8

Medical Malpractice: A Primer

8.1 What is Medical Malpractice?

Medical malpractice is a specific type of professional negligence by a health-care provider. In legal terms, a malpractice claim must prove four key elements: **duty, breach, causation, and damages**. This means that there must have been a doctor-patient relationship establishing a duty of care, the physician must have breached that duty by providing care that fell below the accepted standard of care, that this breach directly caused harm to the patient, and that the patient suffered damages (injuries or losses) as a result. All four elements are required for a malpractice case to succeed – if any element is missing, it is not legally malpractice.

It's important to understand that a poor outcome by itself is not automatically malpractice. Medicine has inherent risks, and not every complication or adverse result is due to physician negligence. For example, a patient might experience a known side effect or complication of a procedure even though the physician did everything correctly. Such an outcome, while unfortunate, is usually not malpractice if the care provided met appropriate standards. In other words, malpractice is about a deviation from the standard of care, not just an unhappy result. A patient's condition can worsen despite proper treatment, or a procedure may have an adverse result, and that alone doesn't imply the doctor was negligent. Malpractice occurs when the physician's actions (or inactions) fell below what a reasonably competent practitioner would have done in the same situation and caused harm.

To illustrate, consider a scenario: A surgeon performs an operation with the same skill and care that most competent surgeons would, but the patient has a rare complication. This is likely a complication, not malpractice, because the surgeon didn't breach the duty of care. In contrast, if a surgeon operates on the wrong site or ignores established safety protocols, and the patient is harmed, that breach of the standard of care could be malpractice if it causes injury. In summary, bad outcomes are not always due to bad medicine – malpractice is specifically when substandard care leads to injury.

8.2 Basic Legal Tenets of Malpractice

Standard of Care: In a malpractice case, much revolves around whether the physician's care met the "standard of care." The standard of care is generally defined as the level and type of care that a reasonably skilled, competent, and prudent physician in the same field would provide under similar circumstances. It's essentially what other typical doctors would do in that situation. This isn't necessarily the best possible care, nor does it require perfect outcomes – it's about what is considered acceptable and appropriate by the medical community. Notably, the standard of care today is usually considered on a national level (in most jurisdictions) rather than a local one, meaning a patient should expect the same basic level of care from a specialist whether they're in a large urban hospital or a small rural clinic. In a lawsuit, the standard of care is established through evidence and often through expert testimony. Doctors practicing in the same specialty (peers) will opine on what a competent physician should or shouldn't have done, and this helps the court determine if there was a deviation. In short, if your care was consistent with what a typical qualified physician would have done, it meets the standard; if it fell below that benchmark, it may be deemed a breach of duty.

Role of Expert Witnesses: Because determining the standard of care and whether it was breached involves medical judgment, expert witnesses play a pivotal role in malpractice litigation. In nearly every malpractice case, both the plaintiff and the defense will hire medical experts (usually physicians in the same field as the defendant) to review the facts and testify about what the appropriate care should have been. These experts explain complex medical issues to the jury in plain language. They answer questions like: What would a reasonably careful doctor have done in this scenario? Did the defendant's actions line up with that, or deviate from it?. Essentially, experts are the ones who define the standard of care for the jury and opine on whether the defendant doctor met it or not. For instance, if a patient had a certain set of symptoms and the doctor failed to order a particular test, an expert might testify that most competent doctors would have ordered that test – indicating a breach. It's important to realize that expert testimony can make or break a case. As a physician, this means that your care will be judged by your peers (in hindsight) and compared to what they say is expected. That's why adhering to well-accepted medical practices and guidelines is so important – it aligns your care with what an expert can defend as the standard. (On the flip side, if an adverse event occurred despite appropriate care, a good expert can explain that to a jury as well.)

Malpractice allegations can arise in any field of medicine, but certain types of claims recur frequently. Understanding these can help you be vigilant in those areas of practice.

- **Diagnostic Errors:** Missed diagnoses or delayed diagnoses are among the most common malpractice allegations. For example, failing to diagnose cancer or a cardiac condition in a timely manner can lead to harm if treatment is delayed. If it's shown that another competent doctor would have recognized the problem or ordered the appropriate tests, a misdiagnosis can be deemed negligent. Diagnostic mishaps often top the list of claims because they can occur in almost every specialty (e.g., a family doctor missing signs of appendicitis or an ER doctor misreading an X-ray).

- **Surgical Mistakes:** Procedural specialists like surgeons face claims related to surgical errors. Classic examples include operating on the wrong site or the wrong patient, leaving a surgical instrument or sponge inside the patient, causing unintended injury to adjacent organs, or failing to control bleeding properly. These are sometimes called "never events" (because they are preventable and should never happen). Even with smaller errors, such as a nicked nerve or vessel, the question will be whether it was an unavoidable risk of the procedure or due to substandard technique. Anesthesia errors also fall in this category – for instance, giving the wrong dose of anesthetic, not monitoring oxygen levels, or mismanaging the airway can lead to severe injury. Because surgical patients are often sedated and can't observe what's happening, documentation and proper protocols (like surgical time-outs to confirm the correct site) are critical to defend care if something goes wrong.

- **Obstetrical Injuries:** OB/GYNs frequently top the lists of sued specialties. Malpractice claims in obstetrics often involve injuries to newborns or mothers during pregnancy or delivery. Examples include failing to perform a timely C-section in the face of fetal distress, improper use of forceps/vacuum leading to a birth trauma, or not recognizing and treating complications like preeclampsia. Such mistakes can result in catastrophic outcomes like brain injury (e.g., cerebral palsy in the infant) or severe hemorrhage/injury to the mother. Because the stakes are so high in obstetrics, juries can be very sympathetic to injured babies/parents, making these claims particularly challenging. Adhering to fetal monitoring protocols and being prepared to act when signs of trouble arise are key risk management practices here.

- **Medication Errors:** Medication-related mistakes are another common source of claims. This can include prescribing or administering the wrong medication or dose, harmful drug interactions, or failing to note an allergy. These errors can happen in any setting – inpatient or outpatient. For instance, an anesthesiologist might administer an incorrect dose of a drug during surgery, or a primary care doctor might prescribe a medication without noticing it conflicts with the patient's other meds. Such errors can cause anything from organ damage to fatal outcomes. Many malpractice cases have arisen from something as simple as a transcription error or illegible handwriting in a prescription (though electronic prescribing has helped reduce that). Always double-checking medications (right patient, drug, dose, route, timing) and maintaining clear communication with pharmacy and nursing staff can prevent these mishaps.

- **Other Common Allegations:** There are many other scenarios that lead to claims – for example, not obtaining informed consent (performing a procedure without explaining the risks to the patient), inadequate follow-up or abandonment (e.g., a consultant failing to communicate critical results to the referring doctor or patient), or procedural complications that were managed poorly (like an infection after surgery that wasn't timely recognized and treated). While these might not be as flashy as a wrong-site surgery, they are frequent causes of malpractice suits. Ultimately, any time a patient is significantly harmed and there's an assertion that something the provider did or didn't do caused it, a malpractice claim can result.

Malpractice liability isn't limited to the individual doctor's actions. Under the legal doctrine of respondeat superior[1], an employer or institution can be held liable for the negligent acts of its employees performed within the scope of their employment. This is known as vicarious liability. In the medical context, this often means a hospital or clinic may be sued (and held responsible) for the actions of the healthcare providers it employs. For example, if a hospital-employed nurse gives the wrong medication dose and harms a patient, the hospital can be named in the lawsuit and made to pay damages, even though it was the nurse's error, because the nurse was acting as the hospital's agent. Similarly, if a physician is a direct employee of a hospital or group, the employer can be vicariously liable for that physician's malpractice.

Importantly, the determination of who is an "employee or agent" can affect liability. Many physicians in hospitals are independent contractors

---

[1]Latin for "let the master answer"

rather than employees – for instance, ER doctors, anesthesiologists, or surgeons might not be direct hospital staff. Generally, employers are only liable for employees, not independent contractors. However, patients often don't know the difference. Courts in some cases have applied an "apparent agency" theory: if a hospital presents a doctor as if they are its staff and a patient reasonably believes that (for example, the patient went to the ER and was treated by a doctor in hospital-branded scrubs, with no idea the doctor was an independent contractor), the hospital may still be held liable for that doctor's negligence. This can vary by jurisdiction, but the takeaway is that from the patient's perspective, they see the hospital as responsible for the care delivered within its walls.

Vicarious liability also applies in clinics or group practices – for instance, a senior physician or a practice owner could be sued for a mistake made by an assistant or trainee under their supervision. Even if you personally did nothing wrong, being a supervising or employing physician means you have a stake in ensuring those working under you are competent and follow proper procedures. While this might sound a bit scary (being on the hook for others' actions), it's usually covered under the organization's or employer's insurance. Hospitals and groups anticipate this and carry malpractice insurance that covers the institution and its staff. Nonetheless, it's a reminder of why good teamwork, protocols, and oversight are important: everyone's actions reflect on the larger entity. In a lawsuit, it's common for plaintiffs to cast a wide net – they might sue the individual doctor, the nursing staff involved, and the hospital itself. From the physician's perspective, if you are an employee, your hospital will likely be a co-defendant (and often they'll help mount a defense). If you're in private practice, be aware that your practice entity (if you have an LLC or corporation) might also be named in a suit in addition to you personally.

In summary, vicarious liability means that not only the person who directly committed the act, but also their employer or institution, can be held responsible. As a physician, this means your actions could implicate your employer, and conversely, you might occasionally find yourself involved in a case due to someone else's error (e.g. a lawsuit against your practice because a partner or employee made a mistake). The concept reinforces the idea that malpractice prevention is a team effort within healthcare settings.

8.3 How to Protect Yourself from Malpractice Claims

No physician can eliminate the risk of a lawsuit entirely, but there are many practical steps you can take to minimize your risk and put yourself in the best defensible position. A lot of malpractice prevention is essentially good medical practice: communicating well, documenting thoroughly, and following safe procedures. Here are some key strategies for protecting yourself.

Practice Excellent Documentation: Good documentation is one of your best defenses if a claim arises. There's a saying in medicine: "If it isn't documented, it didn't happen." In the eyes of a jury (and experts), the medical record is the concrete evidence of what you did and what you were thinking. Thorough, clear notes can demonstrate that you provided appropriate care. On the flip side, sketchy or missing documentation can severely undermine your defense – studies show that inadequate documentation is associated with a significantly higher likelihood of an adverse legal outcome. Always chart pertinent findings, the rationale for your decisions, discussions with the patient (including informed consent or refusal), and follow-up plans. Ensure that entries are timed, dated, and attributable to you. Avoid undocumented verbal orders or hallway advice that doesn't make it into the chart when it influences care. Good documentation isn't just about legal protection – it also improves patient care by enhancing communication among providers. But in court, it's critical: if a step or consideration isn't recorded, a plaintiff's attorney will argue it never happened. So, take the extra minute to write that note or update the chart. It can make all the difference years later in proving the quality of care you gave.

Obtain and Document Informed Consent: Always involve the patient in their care decisions by obtaining informed consent for procedures and treatments, and document that process. Informed consent isn't just a form for the patient to sign – it's a conversation. You should explain the nature of the procedure, its benefits, the significant risks (especially those that a reasonable person would want to know about), and the available alternatives (including doing nothing) in language the patient can understand. Encourage questions and make sure the patient really understands their options. A well-documented informed consent discussion can greatly protect you if a known complication occurs. It shows that the patient was made aware of the risk ahead of time. In fact, a proper consent process enhances patient trust and autonomy, and it can reduce the likelihood of a lawsuit because the patient feels respected and informed. For example, if a patient develops a known side effect of surgery that you discussed beforehand, they're less likely to view it as malpractice and more as an unfortunate risk that materialized. However, remember that informed consent is not a shield against negligence. It protects you only regarding known, disclosed risks – it does not excuse an actual breach of standard of care. In other words, a patient can consent to a procedure's risks, but they are not consenting to you doing it negligently. For instance, if you obtained consent for a surgical procedure including the risk of nerve injury, and the patient unfortunately has a nerve injury, you're in a defensible position if the surgery was done properly and that risk just happened. But if the nerve injury occurred because you operated on the wrong area or used improper technique, consent won't save you – that's not a "risk" of the procedure, that's an error. So, do take consent seriously: tailor the discussion to the patient's situation (generic broad forms are often not enough), and document it in the chart (e.g., "Explained risks X, Y, Z; patient understands and consents"). A well-conducted consent process not only helps legally, it also improves the doctor-patient relationship.

Communicate Openly and Kindly: Strong communication and rapport with patients is perhaps the most powerful tool to prevent lawsuits. Many malpractice suits are driven by patient anger, frustration, or feeling ignored more than by the medical error itself. Patients who feel their physician is honest, caring, and transparent are less likely to resort to litigation even if an adverse outcome occurs. Therefore, make it a practice to listen to your patients, address their concerns, and explain things in plain language. Don't dismiss symptoms or patient input. Simple things like taking a few extra minutes to ensure the patient understands the treatment plan, or even using a bit of empathy and humor, can dramatically improve patient satisfaction. Studies have shown that physicians who are better communicators get sued less often than peers who are more brusque or uncommunicative, despite similar error rates. Also, if something does not go as expected – say the patient has a complication or you make a mistake – do not hide it. It's natural to feel afraid of admitting an error, but patients tend to be more forgiving (and less litigious) when a physician is upfront, apologizes, and tries to make it right. A sincere apology and explanation after an adverse event can defuse anger and prevent a lawsuit in many cases. Many states have "apology laws" that even make such apologies inadmissible as evidence of fault, precisely to encourage open communication. The key is to express empathy ("I'm sorry this happened to you") and, if an error occurred, to take responsibility and explain what will be done to help. Patients often sue because they feel stonewalled or deceived after an injury; avoiding that reaction can protect you. In summary, be the kind of doctor that patients trust – it not only improves care, it also makes them far less likely to see you as an adversary in court.

Understand Your Malpractice Insurance: It's critical to know the basics of your professional liability (malpractice) insurance coverage. Two main types of policies exist: claims-made and occurrence-based. A claims-made policy covers you only if the claim is made (filed) during the period the policy is active (or during an extended reporting period you purchase). This means if you leave a job or switch insurers, you'll typically need to purchase "tail coverage" to cover any claims filed in the future for incidents that happened while you were practicing under the old policy. By contrast, an occurrence policy covers any incident that occurred during the period of coverage, regardless of when the claim is filed. So an occurrence policy automatically covers you for claims that arise later, even after the policy or job has ended. Occurrence coverage is often more expensive, but it offers long-term peace of mind (no need for a tail). Most employed physicians have claims-made coverage through their employer. If you have a claims-made policy, be very mindful about tail coverage when you leave that job or retire – otherwise you could have an uninsured gap. Also, know your policy limits (the maximum it will pay per claim and in aggregate) and whether your policy covers things like legal defense costs in addition to payouts. Notify your insurer promptly if you even suspect a potential claim (for example, if you receive a lawyer's request for records or a notice of intent). Prompt notification is usually required by the policy and ensures they can start your defense early. Finally, consider if your state has any special malpractice environment (caps on damages, etc.) as that can influence how much coverage you should carry. For instance, in states without caps on pain and suffering damages, higher policy limits might be wise. In short, read your insurance policy or talk to your risk manager so you're not caught off guard. The last thing you want is to find out after a lawsuit that you didn't have the right coverage in place.

Maintain Good Practices (Especially for Procedures): Consistently follow safety protocols and engage in ongoing training – these are proactive ways to reduce errors and thus malpractice risk. For procedural specialists, standardized safety checklists are a proven tool. For example, using surgical checklists (like the WHO Surgical Safety Checklist) can prevent critical mistakes. Studies have found that a significant portion of surgical error claims could be mitigated by adhering to such checklists – one review showed nearly one-third of contributing factors in surgical malpractice cases might be avoidable with checklist use. Make it routine to do things like time-outs to confirm the correct patient, procedure, and site, and to double-count sponges/instruments, verify allergies, etc. These mundane steps dramatically cut down on "never events" and improve patient safety, which in turn protects you. Another key area is continual training and simulation, particularly for high-risk scenarios. Practicing emergency protocols (like a code blue, a difficult airway, or an obstetric hemorrhage) in simulated environments with your team can pay off when real life throws a crisis at you. In fact, evidence shows that simulation training can actually reduce malpractice claims. One notable study of obstetricians who underwent simulation-based crisis training saw about a 50% reduction in their malpractice claim rates afterward. The reasoning is simple: better prepared clinicians make fewer critical mistakes under pressure. So, take advantage of simulation drills, CME workshops, or any skills-training relevant to your field. For an anesthesiologist, this might mean sim labs for rare anesthesia complications; for a surgeon, cadaver labs or courses on new techniques; for an ER physician, mock codes or trauma simulations. All these not only improve patient outcomes but can also favorably impact your medicolegal risk. Lastly, know your limits and seek help when needed.

If a case is beyond your expertise, consult a specialist (and document that you did). If you're fatigued or not in the right state to operate, don't push it – patient safety comes first, and recognizing when to pause is itself a risk management act. By staying within the bounds of competent practice and continuously sharpening your skills, you reduce the chances of an error that could lead to a claim.

In summary, protecting yourself from malpractice isn't about practicing "defensive medicine" in the sense of ordering unnecessary tests just to cover yourself. It's more about being diligent, communicative, and cautious in the right ways: chart thoroughly, obtain consent, foster good patient relationships, keep your knowledge and skills up-to-date, follow protocols, and insure yourself properly. These steps not only reduce lawsuit risk – they'll often make you a better clinician overall.

8.4 Curbside Consultations and Malpractice Risk

"Curbside consultations" – the informal asking or giving of medical advice between colleagues without a formal patient evaluation – are a routine part of medical practice. You might call a specialist friend to ask, "Hey, I have this patient with X, Y, Z – what would you do?" or a junior doctor might catch you in the hallway for your opinion on a case. These casual consults can be very useful for patient care and education. However, many physicians wonder: Could I be held liable for advice I give on a patient I'm not formally treating? The answer is generally no, as long as it remains an informal consult, but there are important caveats.

Legal Considerations: Malpractice liability typically requires a physician-patient relationship (duty) to exist. In a true curbside consult, you, as the consultant, have no direct relationship with the patient – you haven't examined them, haven't agreed to treat them, and usually the patient may not even know you were consulted. Because of this, courts have usually found that the consulting doctor in a curbside scenario does not owe a direct duty of care to the patient. In practical terms, this means that if you just offer some informal advice and have no further involvement, it's rare to be named in a lawsuit. Malpractice insurers and literature reports indicate curbside consultants are very seldom sued by patients they never met. So, the overall risk is low, and that's good – otherwise no one would ever informally consult and medicine would become very inefficient.

However, rare doesn't mean never. There have been cases where a curbside consultant did get roped into a lawsuit. This tends to happen if the lines between informal and formal consultation got blurred. For example, if the treating physician documents in the chart, "Discussed with Dr. Smith

(Cardiology) who recommends doing A, B, C," then Dr. Smith's name is now in the record. If the patient later sues, their attorney might say "Who is Dr. Smith? Let's include Dr. Smith in the lawsuit since their advice was part of the decision-making," especially if the advice turned out bad. Being identified in the medical record as providing input significantly increases the chance of being named in a suit. Once you're named, even if you ultimately have a solid defense, you may still go through the hassle of being involved (and needing your own attorney, etc.) until you can be dismissed from the case.

When does an informal consult turn into a liability? The more you actively participate in the patient's care, the more you could be seen as having a doctor-patient relationship (and thus duty). Courts will look at factors like: Did you just give a casual opinion based on a brief description, or did you effectively step into a consulting role? Consider the following red flags that a "curbside" consult is crossing into formal territory:

- You were provided extensive details about the patient's case (history, labs, imaging).
- You personally reviewed the patient's records or tests (like looking at their X-ray or lab results yourself).
- You had any direct interaction with the patient (even a quick bedside peek or talking to them on the phone).
- You recommended a specific plan, treatment, test, or medication (especially if you gave detailed instructions).
- You followed up on the patient's progress or were consulted multiple times about the case.
- You (or your department) billed for your advice or involvement.

If several of these are true, a court might decide that you effectively took on a consulting physician role, implying a physician-patient relationship even without a formal referral. In such instances, both you and the requesting doctor could be considered responsible for the outcome if the advice was wrong or harmful. In fact, there have been malpractice cases where both the treating physician and the informal consultant were sued and the consultant was found partly liable because of the degree of involvement in the patient's care. For example, imagine you're a neurosurgeon and a hospitalist calls you about a patient with neurological symptoms. If you glance at the MRI yourself and say "Oh, that's nothing, no neurosurgery needed" and the patient is discharged and has a bad outcome, you've directly influenced care with a specialist's opinion – a plaintiff could argue you owed a duty at that point.

Risk Mitigation for Curbside Consults: The best way to protect yourself is to keep clear boundaries. If you're the one giving the curbside advice, state the limitations of your input. It's okay to preface: "Without seeing the patient or full work-up, my off-the-cuff impression is ____, but you should use your clinical judgment and consider a formal consult if needed." This sets expectations that you're not taking over the case. Avoid phrases like "I recommend you definitely do X" in an informal consult; instead, you might say "One approach could be X, but again I haven't evaluated the patient." Also, it's wise not to engage in repeated curbside advice on the same complex case – at some point, either formally see the patient or encourage the treating doc to refer. If you find you need to review records or images to give proper advice, that's a sign it should become a formal consult. In a formal consult, you would be properly documenting your findings and recommendations and the patient would likely know about it – which is fine, you're then officially part of the care team. It's the ambiguity that causes trouble, so try not to linger in a gray zone.

From the requesting physician's side, be mindful of how you use curbside advice. Curbside consults should supplement your decision-making, not replace a proper consult when one is indicated. If you do act on a curbside suggestion, document thoughtfully. You might note "Discussed with a specialist informally" without naming if appropriate, or if you name the consultant, make sure it truly was formal enough that they are aware and on board. Remember that if you write "Dr. X said do this," you might inadvertently be inviting scrutiny of Dr. X as well.

True curbside consults carry minimal legal risk – they are usually not considered a doctor-patient interaction for the consultant, so duty doesn't attach in most jurisdictions. But the risk increases if the consultant's involvement deepens. Cases have shown that when a patient is significantly harmed after informal advice, plaintiffs may attempt to sue everyone involved, including the casual consultant. To protect yourself, keep informal consults truly informal: limit advice to general guidance based on the limited info provided, and urge a formal evaluation for anything complex or if you find yourself getting too involved. Many risk managers advise that if a curbside consult goes beyond a quick question, you should convert it to a formal consult (see the patient, document your consultation) to avoid ambiguity. Also, never alter or hide the fact that a conversation took place – honesty is important. If a bad outcome occurs, it's better to clarify your role (or lack thereof) than to pretend you weren't involved after the fact.

Bottom line: Collegial curbside consults are a valuable part of medicine and you shouldn't be afraid to ask or answer a colleague's question. Just be aware of the scope – if you're giving or receiving more than a simple opinion, it may be safer for the patient and for legal purposes to formalize the consultation. By recognizing those situations, you can enjoy the benefit of peer input without unexpectedly joining someone else's lawsuit.

8.5 What to Do If You Are Sued

Despite your best efforts in practice, it's possible that one day you'll be faced with a malpractice lawsuit. Being served with legal papers alleging you harmed a patient can be scary and emotionally distressing. This section will walk you through practical steps to take immediately after being sued, and how to navigate the legal process while taking care of yourself. The good news is that most cases are defensible, and you don't have to go through it alone – you will have a legal team and support. Here's how to approach the situation:

Initial Steps When Served with a Lawsuit: The moment you are served with a summons and complaint (the documents that start a lawsuit), there are a few critical things to do right away:

1. **Contact Your Malpractice Insurer (or Risk Manager) Immediately.** This is your first call, as soon as you've been served (or even if you get a strong indication that a lawsuit is coming). Your malpractice insurance carrier needs to know about the claim so they can start your defense process. They will assign an attorney to represent you (at the insurer's expense) and guide the next steps. Prompt notification is often required by your policy; failing to notify them in a timely manner could even jeopardize your coverage, so don't delay. If you work for a hospital or large practice, you might notify your institution's risk management department and they will coordinate with the insurer. Essentially, raise the flag to the professionals whose job is to help you through this. The sooner your legal team is involved, the better prepared you'll be.

2. **Do Not Discuss the Case with Anyone Except Your Attorney and Insurer.** It is natural to want to vent or explain yourself, but once a lawsuit is filed, a lot of your communications can be legally discoverable by the plaintiff. Do not talk about the case with the patient or the patient's family, and do not attempt to "smooth things over" at this point – that stage has passed once litigation is active. Also, do not speak to the plaintiff's lawyer if they reach out to you. You may get a call from the patient's attorney or an investigator; refer them to your lawyer or insurer. Anything you say to the other side can be used against you out of context. Similarly, be cautious discussing with colleagues: while it's fine to seek emotional support (more on that later), factual details of the case should only be discussed in confidence with your defense team. Conversations about the case with partners, hospital committee members, etc., are generally not protected by attorney-client privilege, and those individuals could be subpoenaed to recount what you said. So, as hard as it is, resist the urge to tell "your side of the story" to others before talking to your lawyer. Once you have an attorney, they will often instruct you on

whom you can or can't talk to about case specifics. An exception to this rule is if you need to speak to a supervisor or hospital counsel as part of internal requirements – typically those communications can be privileged if handled correctly. But as a rule of thumb: mum's the word about case details until your legal counsel directs otherwise.

3. **Secure the Medical Records and Do Not Alter Them.** Obtain a complete copy of the patient's chart (and any other relevant records, such as hospital incident reports) as soon as possible and keep them in a safe place for your review. You will need to familiarize yourself with every detail of what happened. If some time has passed, you might not recall everything – reading the chart will refresh your memory. Just as crucial: do not make any changes or additions to the medical record after the fact. It might be tempting to "clarify" a note or add an addendum once you realize something looks bad or was omitted, but any alteration made post-lawsuit is almost always detected and it will severely damage your credibility in court. In fact, altering medical records can lead to separate legal consequences and can turn a defensible case into an indefensible one. Even something like writing a backdated addendum could be portrayed as a cover-up. So, preserve the records exactly as they are. If there truly is something inaccurate in the chart (say a nurse mis-documented something), discuss it with your attorney – the way to address that is through testimony or clarification in legal proceedings, not by unilaterally fixing the chart after a suit is filed. Also, do not destroy any records. Keep all emails or notes you might have about the case. Intentional destruction (spoliation) of evidence can result in big sanctions. Generally, once a lawsuit is anticipated or filed, you have a duty to preserve all relevant documents.

4. **Cooperate and Communicate with Your Defense Team:** Once your insurer assigns an attorney, you'll typically meet with them (and possibly an insurance claims representative). Be honest and open with your lawyer – remember, attorney-client communications are confidential. Tell them the full story, even parts that might be unflattering. They are on your side and need the truth to defend you effectively. Provide them with any materials or information they request promptly (for example, they might ask for a timeline of events or your personal recollection). It's important to establish a good working relationship: make sure you understand your lawyer's explanation of the process and feel comfortable with their strategy. If you have concerns, voice them. Sometimes, especially in complex cases, you might have input on expert selection or defense approaches. Engaging proactively with your defense can improve the outcome and also help you cope by giving you some sense of control.

Malpractice lawsuits tend to move slowly – they unfold over months and often years. It's important to mentally prepare for a marathon, not a sprint. Here's a brief overview of what happens, so you know what to expect:

- After the complaint is filed and you're served, your attorney will file a response (an "answer") on your behalf, denying the allegations.

- Then comes discovery, which is the fact-finding phase. Both sides exchange information. You will likely be required to give a deposition – this is a sworn out-of-court testimony where the plaintiff's lawyer questions you in detail about the case. It can be nerve-wracking, but your attorney will prepare you extensively for it. You'll review the records and practice answering questions. The key in deposition (and trial) is to stick to the facts and not speculate. Only answer what is asked, truthfully, and don't volunteer extra info. Your lawyer will be there to object to improper questions and guide the process. Likewise, your attorney will depose the plaintiff, other witnesses, and any other doctors involved. Expert witnesses will be identified by both sides and deposed as well.

- There may be independent medical evaluations (if the patient's current condition is relevant), or motions filed (e.g., to try to get the case dismissed or certain evidence excluded). This pre-trial phase can take a long time – sometimes a year or more – with various legal back-and-forth. Throughout this time, don't be surprised if your case gets delayed or continued; court schedules are crowded. It's a slow process, and that's normal.

- Many cases will move toward settlement discussions or mediation at some point. In fact, the vast majority of malpractice lawsuits never go all the way to a jury verdict. Statistics suggest that only around 5–7% of cases end up in a trial; the rest are either dismissed, dropped, or settled out of court. A case might be dropped if discovery reveals it's very weak, or an insurer might settle if they calculate that a reasonable settlement is safer than the unpredictability of a jury. Settlements are not an admission of wrongdoing; often they are business decisions by the insurer.

- If your case does go to trial, it will be a major event, but remember, physicians win the majority of malpractice trials, especially when the evidence of negligence is borderline. Your lawyers and experts will present your defense, and the plaintiff's side will present their case, and a jury (or sometimes a judge) will decide the outcome. Trials can be stressful, but your involvement will primarily be to testify and then leave the legal wrangling to your attorneys.

Throughout this process, keep practicing medicine as normal (unless there's a specific reason you shouldn't). It can be hard to focus, but remember that being sued is not a verdict on your overall abilities or character as a doctor. It can happen to very good physicians. Don't let it consume you – the legal process is largely out of your hands while you're not on the stand. Focus on providing great care to your current patients; many doctors find that continuing to do what they love is a helpful distraction from the lawsuit.

Coping with the Emotional Impact: Being involved in a malpractice suit can exact a heavy emotional toll. It's often described as one of the most stressful experiences of a physician's career. You might feel anger ("How could the patient sue after I tried my best?"), guilt, fear about your reputation or finances, or even shame. Some doctors develop insomnia, anxiety, or depression during litigation. Recognize these feelings as normal – you're not alone in this. It often triggers a sort of grieving process for the trust that was broken. It's crucial during this time to take care of your mental health and seek support.

While you should avoid talking about case specifics, do seek emotional support from trusted individuals. Confide in a close friend, spouse, therapist, or a physician colleague who is not involved in the case, about how you feel. You don't have to discuss the details of the patient's care; you can share the fact that you're going through a lawsuit and it's been hard on you. Bottling it up is not healthy. Many medical societies or hospitals have peer support programs for physicians facing litigation – talking to another doctor who has been through it can be immensely reassuring. They can validate your feelings and remind you that good doctors can get sued and survive it. If you find yourself persistently anxious or depressed, don't hesitate to consult a mental health professional. Sometimes a few sessions with a therapist who understands provider stress, or even short-term medication for anxiety or sleep, can get you through the rough patch. There is no shame in that; it's an accepted part of coping.

One tricky part is that your attorney might advise you not to discuss the case with others, which is sound legal advice regarding facts of the case. But that doesn't mean you cannot tell someone, "I'm under a lot of stress because I'm being sued." You can express your emotions without divulging confidential case details. In fact, psychologists note that having social support is crucial during litigation stress. It helps you maintain perspective and self-worth. Just ensure that whoever you talk to understands the need for confidentiality and is there to support you, not to gossip.

Another aspect of coping is to keep perspective on your identity and competence. A lawsuit can make you doubt yourself as a physician. You might practice more defensively or second-guess decisions. Over time, as you process the experience, try to channel it into learning. Ask yourself if there is anything you could improve (sometimes there is, sometimes it truly was just a bad outcome outside your control). Many doctors come out of litigation feeling wiser or more attentive, which can be a strange silver lining.

But importantly, do not let a case make you feel like you're a "bad doctor." Even excellent doctors get sued – sometimes because of system errors, sometimes because of patient perceptions, and yes, sometimes due to mistakes that any human could make. Recall why you went into medicine and don't let one legal case define you.

Lastly, protect your personal time and wellbeing during this ordeal. Ensure you exercise, get adequate rest, and engage in hobbies or activities that reduce stress. It's easy to let a lawsuit encroach on your every thought. Many physicians describe an omnipresent cloud until the case is resolved. Counteract that by intentionally scheduling enjoyable activities or time with loved ones to give your mind a break. Some find that compartmentalizing the lawsuit (e.g., "I'll think about it only when meeting with my lawyer or preparing, otherwise I put it on a shelf") helps them continue with life. With time, the intensity of emotions often diminishes, especially if you have support.

In conclusion, if you are sued: **do not panic** – take the procedural steps to protect yourself (notify insurer, secure records, limit discussions), work closely with your legal team, and allow yourself to seek support for the emotional aspects. Many, if not most, physicians face a malpractice claim at some point in their career. It's an unfortunate possibility in our profession, but it is something you can get through. By being prepared and understanding the process, you can navigate the legal system more confidently and maintain your professionalism and wellbeing through the challenge. Remember that you're not alone – your colleagues, mentors, and professional organizations can be sources of guidance and comfort. And when it's all over, whether the case is won, settled, or even if there's an unfavorable outcome, you will have gained resilience and insight that can make you an even better physician moving forward.

Chapter 9

Surviving and Thriving in the First 90 Days

The first three months of your new job are a period of intense learning, adjustment, and opportunity. This "orientation" phase can feel like a whirlwind – new names and faces, unfamiliar systems, and the weight of full responsibility on your shoulders. It's normal to feel both excited and overwhelmed. In this chapter, we'll explore strategies to survive and thrive in your first 90 days as a practicing physician. We'll address the transition shock and how to onboard effectively, offer time management tips to keep you afloat, discuss navigating the workplace culture and politics, and guide you in setting 30-, 60-, and 90-day goals that balance immediate performance with long-term growth. By approaching your first 90 days with intentionality, you can build a strong foundation for a successful career.

Embrace the Learner's Mindset: Even though you've finished training, approach your new job as the next stage of learning. Every hospital or clinic has its own way of doing things. In the first weeks, prioritize learning over trying to prove yourself. This means asking questions – lots of them. If you're unsure how to place a referral or what the usual process for a procedure is, ask a colleague or the staff who handles it. People will appreciate that you want to do things correctly. It's far better to ask upfront than to bungle something because you assumed. Remember, you're not expected to know everything on day one. Show humility: phrases like "I'm new here, could you show me how you usually do this?" endear you to staff and signal that you respect their expertise. Most coworkers will be happy to help a newcomer who is polite and eager to learn.

- *Tip:* Carry a small notebook or use a notes app to jot down tidbits you learn (e.g., the direct number for radiology, Mr. Jones in billing who fixes insurance issues, the quirk that clinic X likes faxes instead of emails for consults). These cheat sheets will save you from asking the same question repeatedly and impress others with how quickly you "get" the system.

Build Relationships Early: One of the best ways to integrate into a new culture is to get to know the people – from your fellow physicians to nurses, techs, front desk staff, administrators, and beyond. Early on, take the initiative to introduce yourself. A simple handshake and "Hi, I'm Dr. *, the new* , nice to meet you," in the hallway or breakroom can start things off right. Show genuine interest in others: ask how long they've been with the organization, what they like about working there, etc. People appreciate feeling seen and valued. As you learn names, use them. Something as straightforward as, "Good morning, Maria," to your unit clerk can foster goodwill. As a new physician, you rely on your team for everything from efficient patient care to learning the ropes; earning their trust and goodwill is gold. One practical suggestion is to explicitly ask your new team members about their roles and how you can collaborate best. For instance, "What's the best way for me to communicate orders or preferences to you?" or "How can I make your job easier when we're dealing with a complex patient?" This not only gives you valuable information but also shows colleagues you care about making things work smoothly for everyone. By demonstrating respect and teamwork from the start, you build credibility. Staff will say, "The new doc is great – really considers us," which is exactly what you want.

8 *Tip:* In your first week, learn at least one personal thing about each immediate team member (does the nurse have a hobby? do you share a hometown with the X-ray tech?). Remembering such details (and following up, like "How was your son's soccer game?") shows that you view them as individuals, not just roles. This human connection can set you apart in a very positive way.

Understand the Organizational Landscape: Every workplace has a formal and informal structure. As a newcomer, it's crucial to map out who's who and who does what. Early in your onboarding, get clarity on the chain of command: Who is your direct supervisor or mentor? Who leads your department? Who handles scheduling and who handles clinical operations? Knowing this helps you direct questions or issues to the right person and avoid stepping on toes. Simultaneously, observe the informal networks. Is there a senior nurse who is the go-to for difficult IVs (and also the grapevine source)? Is there an administrative assistant who basically keeps the department running? Identify those key players – often, building rapport with them can smooth your path (they might give you heads-up about issues, or help you cut through red tape). One great strategy is to schedule brief one-on-one meetings with critical individuals in your first month: e.g., the clinic manager, the lead pharmacist, the IT support person. Use that time to introduce yourself, learn about how you'll interface with them, and express that you're looking forward to working together. This proactive approach marks you as someone who's collaborative and respects each person's role.

Adapt to the Culture: "Culture" is the unseen force that dictates how things really get done. Pay attention to the workplace norms. Do doctors and staff socialize or is it very formal? Do emails get answered promptly, or do people prefer phone calls? Is the vibe one of hierarchy or more team-based? In your first 90 days, you are essentially a guest in a new culture – adapt to it before trying to change anything. For example, if most of your colleagues arrive by 7:45am for an 8am start to enjoy coffee together, try to do the same; those casual moments can be important for bonding. If the culture values punctuality for meetings (or alternately, if meetings notoriously start 15 minutes late), knowing that saves you frustration. Also observe how people handle disagreements or give feedback – this will teach you the preferred communication style (some places value direct feedback, others more diplomatic). Avoid making negative comments about how things are done (e.g., "In my residency we had a better system for consults..."). Even if well-intentioned, it can come off as arrogant or as an implication that the current system is inferior. First, master why things are done the way they are; there may be history or constraints you're unaware of. As the saying goes, "learn the rules before you break them." Once you've established yourself (months or a year in), you'll have more capital to suggest improvements – and you'll do so from an informed perspective.

Establish Credibility Through Actions: Especially as a new physician (and perhaps a younger one), you want colleagues and patients to have confidence in you. Credibility isn't assumed – you build it through consistent, reliable actions. Some credibility-builders in the first 90 days include:

- Be on time (or early) for your clinics, rounds, and meetings. Tardiness as the "newbie" is glaring. Reliability in showing up is the simplest trust signal.
- Do what you say you will. If you tell a nurse you'll put in an order or call a consult, do it promptly. If you promise to follow up on a patient's lab, make sure it gets done. Early follow-through sets the expectation that you don't drop balls.
- Admit what you don't know and seek answers. It might feel counterintuitive, but saying "I'm not sure – let me double-check that" can increase others' trust in you. It shows you put patient safety first and have humility. No one will fault a new doctor for asking for help or confirming a dosage; they will fault a doctor who pretends to know and makes a mistake. As one tip from a new physician checklist states: "Don't be afraid to ask for help. You are not expected to know every-

thing... use the resources available to you, including physicians and staff". Colleagues prefer you ask rather than guess and err.

- Handle a crisis or error with grace. Inevitably, something will go wrong – a patient will crash or you'll make a minor mistake. How you react is key. Keep your cool as best as possible, call for backup early if needed, communicate clearly. Afterwards, debrief and learn from it. If staff see that you don't crumble under pressure and you prioritize patient well-being over ego, your stock rises.

Take Advantage of Onboarding Resources: Many organizations provide formal onboarding – orientation sessions, training modules, assigned "buddies" or mentors. Attend all offered trainings, even if they seem mundane or you think you know the material. For example, an EHR training might show specific templates your new group uses (making your documentation easier), or an orientation might explain the org chart. These sessions are also chances to meet other new hires (who could become a support cohort). If you're assigned a mentor or preceptor for the first few weeks, use them! Ask them candid questions about unwritten rules or advice they have for succeeding here. HR might inundate you with info on benefits, insurance sign-ups, etc. – handle those logistical tasks early (don't miss your enrollment deadlines for insurance and retirement plans; stress from an insurance gap is the last thing you need in a new job). Essentially, treat onboarding like a crucial part of your job, not an annoying add-on. It lays the groundwork for everything to come.

Manage Transition Emotions: On a personal level, be prepared for an emotional rollercoaster. It's common to feel "impostor syndrome," wondering if you really are ready to be an attending. You might deeply miss the camaraderie of residency, or conversely feel exhilaration at your newfound autonomy. All of that is normal. It may help to seek out a fellow new physician (maybe someone you met at orientation or a peer from training) to share experiences – you'll realize you're not alone in the feelings. If you have a bad day, remind yourself it gets better with time as you grow more comfortable. And recall that your institution hired you because you are qualified. One of the AAFP tips for new physicians simply states: "Believe in yourself... You have been well-trained and have a great deal to offer your new practice and patients". In other words, trust the process that got you here. When self-doubt creeps in, remember all the challenges you've already overcome (med school, boards, residency) – you are ready for this, and you will get through the learning curve. Confidence (tempered with humility) will come with each passing week.

By focusing on learning, building relationships, and demonstrating reliability in these first weeks, you will gradually transform from "the new doc" to a trusted member of the team. Everyone knows it's an adjustment period, so cut yourself some slack too – you don't have to be perfect, you just have to show up with a positive attitude and willingness to learn. The good habits and rapport you establish in the onboarding phase will pay dividends for years to come.

9.1 Time Management Under Pressure

One of the biggest challenges in your first 90 days (and beyond) is time management. As a new physician, you're expected to provide excellent patient care while juggling paperwork, inbox messages, phone calls, and maybe still learning the computer systems. Initially, everything takes longer – you're not yet fluent in the EHR clicks, you might agonize over charting every detail, and you haven't developed shortcuts for routine tasks. It's easy to feel overwhelmed and end up staying hours late to finish notes. This section provides practical tools for staying efficient and keeping your head above water when the pace is intense. The goal is to work smart so you maintain quality of care and your sanity.

Optimize Your Documentation Workflow

Charting and notes can consume a huge chunk of your day if not managed. A few strategies to streamline:

Use Templates and Smart Phrases: Most EHRs allow you to create templates for common visit types (annual physicals, diabetic checkups, preop evaluations, etc.). Invest time up front to set these up. For example, during flu season you might have a template for a routine flu visit with fields for vaccine lot and common advice – this can save time on each patient. Templates ensure you don't forget key questions and reduce repetitive typing. Just be careful to update any template text to fit the specific patient (avoid the cut-and-paste trap of leaving irrelevant info in a note). Similarly, use smartphrases or macros for common chunks of text. If you often write "patient instructed to call for any fever >101 or worsening pain," make that a shortcut. The more you automate routine documentation, the more mental energy you free for complex thinking. As one efficiency resource says, templates are great for routine visits with standard queries. Also consider creating default ordersets for common scenarios (e.g., chest pain workup orderset) to save time clicking each component.

Document in Real-Time (or Close to It): It's tempting to see patients back-to-back and save notes for later, but this can lead to a daunting pile of charts at day's end (the infamous "note bloat" or spending your evening in the EHR). A recommended approach is to complete most documentation during the encounter or immediately after. For instance, some physicians dictate or type their assessment and plan in front of the patient – summarizing out loud what the plan is. This not only finishes the note faster, but also reinforces understanding with the patient (two birds, one stone). You might say, "Okay Ms. Lee, to summarize: you came in with X, on exam Y, I think it's Z. So I'll prescribe medication A and order test B. We'll follow up in 2 weeks." While saying that, you're simultaneously writing it in the chart. Patients often appreciate the recap, and you leave the room with the bulk of your note done. Even if you can't do the whole note in the room, try to chart the history and exam in between patients when possible, so you're left mainly with the plan to finalize later. Avoid procrastinating on notes – the fresher the memory, the quicker the note.

Know When to Stop Writing: Perfectionism can kill efficiency. Sure, your residency taught you thorough documentation, but in practice, you need to find a balance. Not every visit needs a novel. Be clear and concise. If it's a straightforward follow-up on a stable condition, a brief note focusing on interval changes and plan is sufficient. Remember that not every box in the EHR needs to be clicked. Focus on medically relevant documentation rather than documenting for documentation's sake. Over-documenting not only wastes time but can make important info hard to find. One tip is to familiarize yourself with billing requirements for common visit codes (E/M guidelines) – once you know what's required for a level 3 vs level 4 visit, you won't overdo documentation. For example, a routine follow-up might not need a comprehensive review of systems – so don't spend time filling one out if it's not clinically necessary. Give yourself permission to "let go of perfection" in notes. Aim for accuracy and adequacy, not literary prose.

Tame the Inbox and Calls

Many new physicians are caught off guard by how much non-visit work there is – lab results to review, patient messages, prescription refills, forms to sign, consult reports, etc. The key is not letting the inbox rule you.

Set Aside Inbox Time: Instead of constantly interrupting yourself to check emails or messages with each notification (which kills concentration), designate specific times in the day for inbox processing. For example, plan 20 minutes mid-morning and mid-afternoon to tackle messages, plus a final check before leaving. During those times, focus and clear as much as possible. Outside those times, unless something urgent pops up, give yourself permission to not look at the inbox. This batching can significantly improve efficiency.

Triaging and Delegating: Not everything in the inbox needs you personally. Work with your team to filter and delegate what you can. Nurses or medical assistants can handle a lot of routine messages – for instance, normal lab results calls, scheduling follow-ups, medication refill protocols. Many practices implement a system where messages are categorized: ones requiring physician input vs. ones that staff can handle vs. ones that are FYI or irrelevant. If your practice doesn't have this, talk to your office manager about setting up some triage rules. Commonly, refill requests, referral requests, and general patient questions can often be handled by staff following standing orders or protocols. For example, a nurse could handle a request for a blood pressure medication refill for a stable patient by checking if labs are up to date and then forwarding to you just for quick co-signature. Also, ask to unsubscribe or filter out non-essential messages (newsletters, non-urgent FYI notes) so they don't clutter your view. The AMA advises routing certain info like routine hospital progress notes or low-importance notifications away from the physician's primary inbox. The leaner your inbox, the quicker you can address what truly needs your attention.

Utilize Quick Actions: Have canned responses for frequent message types. If you find yourself typing the same explanation to patients (e.g. diet advice for high cholesterol or follow-up instructions for lab work), create a template response you can tweak and send. Some EHRs let you save phrases or use dot phrases for patient communications too. This speeds up messaging.

Phone Calls: For calls that require you to call a patient back, try to batch those as well, maybe toward the end of the day, unless truly urgent. Keep a running list so you can knock them out in one sitting. Before calling, quickly review the chart so you have answers ready (saves you from having to call them back again after looking something up). If you have a particularly heavy call-back load, see if any could be converted to visits or handled by a nurse call (sometimes patients call with things that really need an appointment; don't be afraid to have staff schedule them to see you).

In some settings, you might have an option to get a scribe or use voice recognition software. If documentation is a major pain point and those resources are available, consider them. Medical speech-to-text has improved; dictating an assessment may be faster for you than typing, especially if you're not a fast typist. A number of physicians find that using scribes or voice tech drastically cuts down their charting time.

Prioritize and Plan Your Day

At the start of each day (or the night before), take a moment to plan. Review your schedule – identify any complex patients or double bookings that might require extra time. If you anticipate a tough case, maybe arrange for a lighter load around it or inform your nurse that you might run behind and to pad the next slot. Prioritization is key when everything seems urgent. A useful approach is the Eisenhower Matrix mindset: figure out what's urgent and important (must be done today), what's important but not urgent (schedule it), what's urgent but not important (delegate it if possible), and what's neither (consider dropping it). For example, signing that pre-op form for tomorrow's surgery is urgent and important (do it today). Reading the entire 20-page hospital policy manual – important for general knowledge but not urgent (schedule time later in the month). A patient's portal message asking about an OTC medication – important to them but not an emergency (could be delegated to nurse or answered at day's end). By sorting tasks mentally, you ensure the critical stuff isn't lost and you don't waste prime energy on low-value tasks.

Use Technology and Tools

Simple tools can save you a lot of time. Use your calendar not just for meetings but to block focus time (e.g., block 30 minutes at lunch to catch up on charts or to eat!). If your clinic allows, adjust your schedule template during the first weeks – maybe book yourself a short break after every 3-4 patients to catch up on notes until you get more efficient. Some EHRs have analytics to show your chart completion times or inbox stats; review those to self-audit where time sinks are. If you find you're consistently spending an hour on charts after work, try to pinpoint why – are you seeing too many patients too soon? Are you being overly detailed? Identifying the cause can suggest solutions (like more template use, or talking to your chief about schedule expectations). Also, consider time-tracking for a day or two: jot down what you do in a given hour. You might discover, for example, that you spend 30 minutes searching for information (maybe you need more orientation on the EMR) or that you get interrupted frequently (maybe you can set a policy with staff to batch non-urgent questions). Sometimes small changes (like having the medical assistant pre-load the day's lab results into your note beforehand) can save you minutes that add up.

Guard Your Personal Time

Part of time management is avoiding burnout by not letting work bleed endlessly into off-hours. In the first 90 days, you'll likely have some longer evenings catching up, but set boundaries early. Maybe decide that by 7 pm you stop checking the work email, or that you won't sacrifice all your weekends – keep at least one day work-free if possible. Discuss with family or friends about this intense period and enlist their support (they'll understand if you're a bit scarce, but also they can remind you to rest). As you streamline your workflow with the tips above, aim to leave work at work more and more. Efficiency isn't just about seeing more patients – it's about finishing your tasks in a reasonable time so you can recharge and come back tomorrow at your best.

Improving time management is an ongoing process. Don't hesitate to ask colleagues for their favorite efficiency hacks – physicians love trading these tips ("Oh, you didn't know, you can auto-import the med list with .medlist phrase!"). Over the first 90 days, you'll likely cut down your charting time significantly as you become familiar with the system and develop your own shortcuts. The important thing is to be proactive: recognize when you're struggling and try new strategies to fix it, rather than just feeling constantly behind. With good time management habits, you'll not only get your work done faster but also reduce stress, making you a more present and happier doctor for your patients.

Navigating Organizational Dynamics

No matter how excellent a clinician you are, thriving in a new job also requires political and organizational savvy. "Organizational dynamics" refers to the unwritten rules, power structures, and social politics that exist in every workplace. As a newcomer, you step into a pre-existing web of relationships and hierarchies. Early missteps here can create friction, while understanding how to work within the system will help you avoid landmines and get things done effectively. This section will help you decode your new workplace's dynamics, identify key stakeholders, and steer clear of common pitfalls in office politics.

Learn the Hierarchy and Key Players: Early on, clarify the formal hierarchy. Know who your boss is – is it the department chair, the medical director, the clinic owner? – and what their expectations are. If you have multiple roles (clinical, teaching, research), clarify with each supervisor how your time and priorities should be balanced. Also, identify the influential figures beyond your direct boss. Often, long-tenured staff or senior physicians carry a lot of informal influence. For example, the senior nurse who's been there 20 years might not have a big title but everyone listens to her – if she gives you advice, heed it, and if you win her support, she can be your advocate. Pay attention in meetings to who are the frequent talkers or decision-shapers. It might help to sketch a quick org chart for yourself with names and titles, and jot a note about each person (e.g., Dr. A – head of QI committee, or Joan – office manager, good person to ask about scheduling issues). Knowing who does what and who holds power ensures you direct your questions/requests appropriately. For instance, if you want a change in the clinic workflow, proposing it to the office manager (who can implement it) will be more fruitful than offhand complaining to a random colleague.

Build Alliances with Support Staff: Your relationships with non-physician staff can significantly impact your success. Medical assistants, nurses, schedulers, billing specialists – these folks actually run the engine of patient care. Treat them as valued teammates. If they see you as respectful and team-oriented, they will likely go the extra mile to help you. Conversely, if a new doctor is dismissive or rude, staff may do the bare minimum for them (or worse, gossip about them). Simple courtesies like saying please and thank you, learning names, and acknowledging good work ("Thanks for getting that IV so quickly!") set a positive tone. Also, learn their workflows – spend a little time understanding how the front desk handles calls or how the lab tech processes specimens. The insight will help you empathize and collaborate better (e.g., you'll know not to double-book add-on patients at 4:45 because the front desk has end-of-day tasks and it creates strain). When staff see that you "get" their challenges, they'll view you as an ally rather than just another demanding doctor. This goodwill is invaluable if you need help on a hectic day or a favor down the line.

Communication is Key: In any organization, misunderstandings can lead to conflict. Early on, clarify how you should communicate with various stakeholders. For example, if you're a hospitalist, is it expected to call the primary care doctor after you see their patient, or just send a note? If you're in a group practice, do physicians text each other for quick consults, or is email preferred? Matching the communication norms will help you integrate smoothly. When in doubt, err on the side of more communication rather than less – keep your supervisor informed of any significant developments or issues ("We had a minor OR incident today, here's what happened, just FYI"). They'll appreciate being in the loop and see you as transparent. Never assume someone else has communicated something – a common pitfall is thinking "Oh, I figured the nurse would tell the manager about the issue" and then it falls through cracks. If it's important, follow up yourself or confirm it was done.

Additionally, start building a professional network within the organization. That means forging good working relationships not just in your immediate unit but also with consult services, ancillary departments (pharmacy, PT, radiology). Introduce yourself to the pharmacist who calls with a med interaction – they'll remember you next time and perhaps handle it more collaboratively. Thank the social worker who found a rehab bed for your patient. These small interactions build your reputation internally as a team player.

Avoid Office Politics and Gossip: Office politics can be tricky – as a newbie, it's wise to stay neutral on any longstanding internal rivalries or cliques. You might notice some physicians complain about others, or one group blaming another department for issues. As a new person, do not take sides or join in the blame game, no matter how tempting it is to bond with a group by agreeing. Politely steer clear or stay non-committal: "I haven't been here long enough to know, but I'm sure everyone's trying their best." Similarly, if someone tries to pull you into gossip about a colleague's personal life or competence, it's safest to not engage. What you say will get around. You want the word about you to be about your good work, not "the new doc was talking smack about so-and-so." Keep your conversations professional. Over time, you'll discern which colleagues are trustworthy confidants vs. which tend to stir drama. Gravitate to the positive, solution-oriented folks.

Learn the Conflict Resolution Pathways: Despite best efforts, conflicts can arise – maybe a misunderstanding with a nurse, or friction with a colleague over patient management. Learn how your organization handles this. Some places encourage direct physician-to-physician discussion; others want a supervisor or mediator involved sooner. When a conflict arises, address it in a timely, professional manner. For example, if a consultant consistently delays seeing your patients, instead of blasting them in a note or email, have a direct conversation or involve your attending lead to help mediate. Approach conflicts with curiosity and collaboration: "I noticed X has been happening; I wanted to understand if there's something on our end contributing, and how we can improve this." This non-accusatory style can turn a potential feud into a problem-solving session. Also, don't let resentment fester – many small issues can be cleared up with one honest talk. Early in your tenure, it might feel intimidating to confront a problem (especially if the person is senior to you), but doing so professionally shows confidence and prevents larger issues later.

Be Mindful of Boundaries: Navigating dynamics also means understanding professional boundaries. As a new hire, you might be closer in age to some staff than other doctors, which could lead to a false sense of informality. Friendly relationships are great, but remember lines – for instance, becoming too chummy or flirty with staff can lead to perceptions of favoritism or worse, harassment claims. Maintain respectful boundaries. Similarly, use discretion in social media – avoid connecting with direct coworkers on personal social platforms right away; keep things professional until you've established appropriate friendships over time.

Utilize Mentors": If you're lucky, your department might assign a mentor to help acclimate you. Use them as a resource to decipher the political landscape. You can ask, "Hey, I'm noticing some tension between X and Y departments, anything I should know?" or "How does our group usually handle when someone wants to change a workflow?" They can give you the historical context and advise on the best approaches. If no formal mentor, find an informal one – perhaps a young physician who joined a year or two ago (they remember what it's like and can warn you of pitfalls they encountered) or a well-respected senior doc who is approachable. It's often said that success in an organization is 50% what you do and 50% how you navigate the system; a mentor can teach you the latter.

Early Wins Without Stepping on Toes: You likely come brimming with ideas and wanting to make an impact (which is great!). The first 90 days, however, are usually about learning and integrating, not grand revolutions. Still, you can achieve some "quick wins" that help the organization and show your value, without ruffling feathers. Focus on improvements that are within your sphere of control and relatively uncontroversial. For instance, maybe you notice the discharge instruction template is outdated

– you quietly update it and share with the group, saving everyone time. Or a storage room is chaotic – you organize it one afternoon. Small wins like these solve minor pain points and demonstrate initiative. Just ensure to communicate appropriately (don't overhaul a protocol without permission; but tidying up, or suggesting a new workflow for something minor, is usually welcome). When people see you contributing positively right away, they'll embrace you faster. It also builds confidence – yours and others' in you.

Know When to Say No (Tactfully): In the enthusiasm of being new, you might be inclined to say yes to every request or committee. However, overcommitting is a danger. It's okay, even wise, to pace yourself. If in your first month the practice manager asks you to also take charge of some task (like "Will you be the lead for clinic scheduling optimization?"), it's fine to express that you're still getting your bearings and would prefer to contribute once you've settled (or take on something smaller first). People will respect a thoughtful "no" more than a yes that leads you to burn out or do a subpar job. One of the new physician tips is exactly this: "It is OK, and wise, to hold off on committing to too many tasks until you are sure of the time your primary responsibilities will require.". Early on, under-promise and over-deliver. Protect your time and energy so you can excel at your core duties. Once you've found your rhythm (after a few months), you can gradually step up involvement in extras.

Navigating organizational dynamics comes down to situational awareness and interpersonal skills. Pay attention, listen more than you speak at first, respect everyone, and steer clear of unnecessary drama. By doing so, you'll build a reputation as someone who is easy to work with and a positive addition to the team. A well-navigated first 90 days means you've not only learned your job, but you've figured out how to get things done within your new "ecosystem" – an important factor for long-term success and job satisfaction.

9.2   Setting Personal and Professional Goals

The first 90 days are not just about treading water – they're also about setting the course for your growth and success in this new chapter. Amidst all the immediate responsibilities, it's valuable to carve out time to plan your short-term and long-term goals. Having a 30-60-90 day plan can provide structure to your transition and ensure you're making progress on multiple fronts: patient care, efficiency, self-development, and laying the groundwork for future ambitions. Rather than just letting the days fly by, being intentional with goal setting will help you stay focused and measure your success.

Why 30-60-90 Days? The concept of a 30-60-90 day plan is commonly used for new hires. It breaks the nebulous "first few months" into concrete phases with specific objectives. In essence, it's a roadmap for your onboarding period. By defining what you want to accomplish in the first 30 days, 60 days, and 90 days, you create manageable targets that align with both short-term needs and long-term integration. This helps you adjust quickly and effectively. Such a plan should cover learning goals (e.g., mastering systems or knowledge gaps), performance goals (e.g., achieving a certain patient load or clinic flow efficiency), and personal goals (e.g., work-life balance habits). Importantly, make sure your goals tie into the organization's expectations and your role's duties – you want to meet or exceed what's expected of a new physician in your position.

Let's outline a sample framework:

First 30 Days – "Learning and Settling In":

Goals: Focus on learning the ropes and building relationships.

- **Understand all major workflows:** By Day 30, be comfortable with the EHR for notes, ordering, messaging, and know how to navigate the hospital/clinic for key tasks (admitting patients, consulting other services, scheduling follow-ups, etc.). A concrete goal might be "independently perform X task without help." If your first week you needed help to discharge a patient in the system, aim that by week 4 you can do it solo.
- **Meet every key colleague/stakeholder:** Make sure in the first month you've personally met all physicians in your department, your direct support staff, and any frequent contacts (like the referral liaison or the unit manager). Perhaps set a goal to have a brief 1:1 chat with each senior partner or each member of your immediate team. Networking internally early on will pay off.
- **Achieve baseline patient care metrics:** By end of 30 days, you might aim to be seeing [X]% of a full patient load. For instance, if full load is 20 patients a day, maybe aim for 10-12 by week 4 (depending on your field). Similarly, goal could be "ensure no more than 2 charts open at end of each day" by Day 30, to prevent note backlog – essentially establishing good habits.
- **Identify areas for improvement:** As you learn, note where you struggle. Maybe you realize you need to brush up on billing codes or a certain procedure. A goal can be to address one of those – e.g., complete a quick review or CME on that topic by end of month.
- **Personal goal:** Establish at least one work-life boundary or routine. For example, commit to leaving by a certain time twice a week to attend an exercise class or have dinner with family. Or make a goal to explore one new thing in the city if you relocated (to integrate personally).

Days 31-60 – "Increasing Independence and Efficiency":

Goals: Start adding volume/responsibility, improve efficiency, and contribute to the team.

- **Ramp up patient volume or duties:** By Day 60, aim to handle a workload closer to full capacity (maybe 80% of full volume). If you were double-booked with a preceptor initially, perhaps now you're seeing your own patients completely. Or if you're a surgeon, by week 8 you might aim to schedule and perform your first solo surgeries or fill your OR block. Essentially, transition from orientation mode to regular productivity mode.
- **Time management improvements:** Identify one or two efficiency targets and meet them. For example: reduce average time writing a clinic note to 5 minutes (using templates) by practicing each day. Or clear the inbox by day's end 90% of days. Or start charting in real-time for every patient by the 60-day mark. Small measurable goals like "complete all notes by 6pm each day for two weeks straight" can motivate you and show progress.
- **Enhance clinical skills/knowledge:** Perhaps set a goal to attend a CME lecture or grand rounds once a week, or finish reading a clinical guideline relevant to your practice. Alternatively, if you have boards or certification, dedicate time each week to study. By 60 days, maybe complete a certain number of board questions or chapters. Continuing to invest in your knowledge will make you more confident at work.
- **Strengthen relationships and visibility:** At this stage, you're not brand-new, so start engaging more. Goal examples: speak up at least once in each department meeting (ask a question or offer a comment). Join a hospital committee or attend a medical staff meeting to start integrating into the broader organization. Perhaps volunteer to present a short topic at noon conference or contribute to a newsletter – something that shares your expertise and raises your profile. Don't overdo it, but one well-chosen involvement can both showcase your strengths and help you meet more colleagues.
- **Feedback checkpoint:** Around the 2-month mark, it's smart to seek feedback. Set a goal to have a brief check-in with your supervisor or mentor by day 60. Ask how you're doing, any areas to improve, and whether you're meeting expectations. This shows initiative and helps correct course if needed. For instance, your chair might say you're doing great clinically but need to close charts faster – better to know and fix it now than at a formal evaluation.
- **Personal goal:** By 60 days, hopefully you feel more settled. Set a wellness goal: maybe establish a regular exercise routine, or schedule your needed medical appointments (doctors often neglect their own health during busy transitions), or plan a weekend getaway to recharge after two intense months. Taking care of yourself is a goal

too – a healthy, happy physician provides better care.

Days 61-90 – "Solidifying and Looking Forward":

Goals: By three months, you should be functioning fully in your role. Now it's time to consolidate gains, aim for any remaining performance metrics, and lay groundwork for future projects.

- **Achieve full productivity:** By day 90, aim to be at the expected patient load or OR cases or teaching load for your role. You should be handling call or rotations as scheduled. In short, you're now a fully contributing member of the team. If there are still aspects you feel hesitant about (like a certain clinic procedure or managing clinic flow on double-book days), focus on mastering those now.
- **Quality and Performance Goals:** With baseline efficiency under control, ensure you're also delivering quality. Maybe set a goal to review a few cases for quality improvement – check that your documentation meets billing requirements, or that your patient outcomes (blood pressure control rates, etc.) are on track. Some organizations track new physician metrics (like patient satisfaction scores). If you have access to any performance data, use it to self-improve. For example, if patient feedback says "doctor didn't explain medication side effects," you might incorporate a better script into your visits by day 90.
- **Initiate a longer-term project:** The first 90 days are also about setting direction for your ongoing growth. Think about a larger goal you have – maybe research, or starting a new clinical program, or taking on a leadership role in some capacity. By the end of 90 days, take one concrete step toward that. For instance, if research is your interest, by day 90 you could connect with the research office or identify a potential project and mentor. If you want to build a niche practice, maybe start marketing internally ("By the way, I have an interest in sports medicine if anyone has patients that might benefit"). Or if teaching is a goal, volunteer to give a lecture to residents next quarter. Also, discuss with your leadership about your future plans – as one tip recommends, share your 1-5-10 year plan with them to ensure your current work aligns with your goals. This helps them help you; for example, if they know you aim to become an ultrasound guru, they might assign you to an ultrasound course next.
- **Solidify relationships:** By now you have a sense of who your close allies and mentors are. Keep nurturing those relationships. Also, if there were any strained relationships or unresolved issues from earlier, address them. You want to end the 90 days with a clean slate and strong network. You might also seek out a professional development conversation with your boss: "Now that I've been here 3 months, I'm eager to continue growing – what do you suggest I focus on in the

next 6-12 months?" This shows ambition and openness to guidance.

- **Reflect and Adjust:** A key goal at 90 days is to evaluate your progress. Look back at your initial goals – did you meet them? Where did you excel, and where do you still struggle? Perhaps you met the clinical targets but at the expense of personal time – that's a signal to work on work-life balance in the next phase. Or maybe you did great with team integration but feel clinically there's more to learn in a certain area – plan some CME or mentorship for that. Write down your wins (it's important to acknowledge how far you've come in just 3 months!) and identify 2-3 goals for the next quarter. This habit of periodic self-assessment will keep you on a growth trajectory.

In creating and executing your 30-60-90 day plan, remember to make your goals SMART: Specific, Measurable, Achievable, Relevant, Time-bound. For example, "improve documentation" is vague, but "complete all clinic notes by 6pm on the same day for the next month" is SMART. Share some of your goals with your supervisor to ensure they're on the right track – they might have input on what's realistic or important. Also share with a mentor or peer for accountability.

Balancing patient care, efficiency, self-development and long-term growth is like juggling – you can't give 100% to each at every moment, but across 90 days you can allocate attention to all. Some weeks you'll focus more on just getting through the clinic day (immediate patient care), other times you'll have a moment to attend a conference (self-development), other times you might initiate a future project (long-term). The plan ensures you don't neglect any one area for too long.

By setting and meeting your 90-day goals, you'll hit the ground running in your new job. You'll show your employer that you're proactive and goal-oriented, and you'll prove to yourself that you can thrive in this new environment. Moreover, you'll have laid a solid foundation for the rest of your first year – with good habits, strong relationships, and clear directions for growth. The first 90 days are just the beginning, but they set the tone for the journey ahead. With intentional planning and reflection, you'll not only survive this challenging period – you'll truly thrive.

Appendix A

Sample wRVU Calculation

Here's an example of how work RVUs translate to compensation in an offer:

Dr. X has a contract offering $45 per wRVU with a base salary of $200,000 per year for the first 5,000 wRVUs, and then $45 for each wRVU beyond 5,000 (paid as quarterly bonus).

In year 1, Dr. X generates 5,500 wRVUs. They would earn base $200,000 + bonus for 500 extra RVUs = $22,500, total $222,500.

The next year, no base guarantee, purely $45/RVU. If they do 6,000 RVUs, they get $270,000. If only 4,500 RVUs, $202,500 (and perhaps there's a minimum salary floor or not – ideally the contract ensured year 2 base minimum as well).

Always ask how the conversion factor compares to national benchmarks and if there are thresholds. Ensure you know if things like vacation or administrative time have any RVU credit or not (usually not).

As a quick mental check: if you know common CPT RVUs, you can estimate workload. E.g., if you're an internist, a mix of 99213 (1.3 RVU) and 99214 (1.92 RVU) visits – say average ~1.5 RVU per visit – to hit 5,000 RVUs, you'd need ~3,333 visits/year (~64/week). Is that doable given your clinic template? Factor such calculations in evaluating targets.

Appendix B

Contract Review Checklist

Before signing, go through this list:

- ☐ Compensation details are clear: Base salary, bonus structure, any draw/forgiveness, timing of payments – all specified. Examples given if formula is complex.

- ☐ Duties and schedule documented: Clinic hours, call expectations, any specific obligations (like outreach clinics, admin roles) are either stated or reasonably outlined.

- ☐ Call terms acceptable: Frequency and any compensation or comp time defined. No excessive or unfair burden on you relative to others.

- ☐ Malpractice and tail understood: Policy type (claims vs occurrence) known. Tail coverage responsibility is addressed and you're comfortable with it (or have a plan).

- ☐ Non-compete reasonable: Geographic area and duration won't unduly hamstring your career. Ideally not enforced if you're terminated without cause.

- ☐ Termination clauses fair: Notice period for both parties, any penalty for early resignation, and any "we can terminate you early if you resign" clauses are acceptable or removed.

- ☐ Benefits and perks confirmed: All important benefits (health, retirement match, CME, time off, loan repay, signing bonus, relocation) that were promised are included in the contract or offer letter. Check any payback provisions on bonus/relocation (usually prorated over a couple years).

- ☐ Partnership/promotions addressed (if relevant): If applicable, time-line or criteria for partnership or title advancement is mentioned or at least not contradictory to what was discussed.

- ☐ No surprising clauses: Read for anything like indemnification, arbitration, or exclusive employment clauses. Ensure you can live with them. E.g., if you planned on moonlighting, does contract allow it or do you have written permission?

- ☐ Legal review done: A healthcare contract attorney (or at least a knowledgeable mentor) has looked it over and pointed out any issues, and those have been resolved or you accept them.

- ☐ All blanks filled and no contradictory attachments: Sometimes contracts reference an appendix (e.g., a compensation plan document) – make sure you have it. No "[to be determined]" blanks left unaddressed.

- ☐ Your gut feeling is positive: Finally, beyond the paper, do you feel this employer has been transparent and fair? If any interactions felt off, did you resolve them? You want to enter the job with confidence in the people as well as the contract.

About the Author

Dr. Matthew Segar is a board-certified cardiologist and current electrophysiology fellow at the Texas Heart Institute (THI). He earned his medical degree from the Indiana University School of Medicine and completed his Internal Medicine residency at UT Southwestern before pursuing advanced cardiovascular training at the THI. Recognized for his works on machine learning in heart failure and cardiovascular disease management management, Dr. Segar has received accolades from both the National Institutes of Health (NIH) and the American Heart Association (AHA). Drawing from his own experience navigating the complex process of securing his first attending position, as well as insights gathered from colleagues across the field, Dr. Segar provides a practical roadmap for early-career physicians embarking on this important career transition.

For More Resources

For additional resources or to contact the author, visit:
www.segar.me

www.ingramcontent.com/pod-product-compliance
Lightning Source LLC
Chambersburg PA
CBHW050508210326
41521CB00011B/2370